The Case for
Servant Leadership

By Kent M. Keith

ROBERT K. GREENLEAF
CENTER FOR
SERVANT LEADERSHIP

Printed in the United States of America.

Book and cover design by Joe Hunt
Second Edition

THE CASE FOR
SERVANT
LEADERSHIP

BY KENT M. KEITH

SECOND EDITION

To the memory of
Robert K. Greenleaf
(1904-1990)
whose essay on
"The Servant as Leader"
changed my life
and the lives of millions of others

Contents

Preface to the Second Edition

I am grateful to all those who provided positive feedback regarding the first edition of *The Case for Servant Leadership*. During the past four years it has been used by a wide range of individuals as well as businesses, government agencies, non-profit organizations, hospitals, schools, and more than forty universities.

The Case for Servant Leadership was written as a short introduction or orientation to servant leadership that could also serve as a resource or springboard for those who wish to explore further. In this new edition, I have added several quotations and a few more examples of servant-leaders. I have updated the text with paragraphs summarizing scholarly definitions of servant leadership and recent research on the impacts of servant leadership in the workplace. In response to inquiries, I have created an appendix on servant leadership compared with other ideas or theories of leadership. Finally, I have added a list of sources. It is my hope that these changes will enhance the usefulness of the book for those who wish to read more.

It is also my hope that if you wish to know more about servant leadership, you will contact the Greenleaf Center for Servant Leadership (www.greenleaf.org). The Center provides publications, conferences, seminars, distance learning courses, and intensive training workshops. I encourage you to become a member of the Center, make use of its resources, meet others on the servant leadership journey, and support the worldwide servant leadership movement.

K.M.K.
June 2012

Preface to First Edition

This book is about creating a better world. There does not have to be so much pain and suffering, so much war and violence, so much starvation and disease, so many crushed dreams and untapped talents, so many problems unsolved and so many opportunities ignored. *The world does not have to be like this.*

One reason the world is like this is that people are using the power model of leadership. The purpose of this book is to make the case for the service model of leadership. It is the most ethical, relevant, practical, and effective model of leadership that I know. It is also the model of leadership that is the healthiest and most meaningful for those who lead.

Those who live the service model are called servant-leaders. This book is not an impartial assessment of servant leadership, nor a survey of the literature on servant leadership. It is about the why and how of servant leadership. It is the case for servant leadership argued by an advocate. During the past thirty years, I have served in managerial and leadership roles in the public sector, the private sector, the academic sector, and the non-profit sector. I have seen the pain and destruction that result from the power model of leadership, and I have been inspired by the humanity and effectiveness of the service model. I have no doubt that the world will be a better place when more leaders and organizations practice servant leadership.

I also have no doubt that servant leadership is best for the leader. It is the most meaningful, satisfying way to lead. It is not about self-denial or self-sacrifice. It is about *self-fulfillment*. Servant-leaders find a kind of deep happiness that is not available to other kinds of leaders.

While I am convinced that servant leadership is the best form of leadership, each person must decide for himself or herself. Such a decision often comes after a great deal of thought and experience. I have provided questions at the end of the book to stimulate individual reflection and group discussion. My hope is that each reader will not only decide to become a servant-leader, but will decide to take action—now!

K.M.K.
January 2008

1.

It Starts with the Desire to Serve

The modern servant leadership movement in America was launched by Robert K. Greenleaf. In 1970 he published his essay, *The Servant as Leader,* in which he coined the phrase "servant leadership." Greenleaf said that servant leadership begins with "the natural feeling that one wants to serve."[1]

I believe that most of us do, in fact, want to serve. When we look deeply into ourselves, most of us discover that we truly care about people, and want to make a positive difference in their lives. This "better nature" may take time to emerge, and even when it does, it can be crowded out by the pressures of daily life. But it is there. We can still hear the call of service, and we can respond.

In his book, *The Call of Service*, Robert Coles described his interviews with people who answered that "call within." One of them was Dion Diamond, a young black college student in the early 1960s who went to Louisiana to work on voter registration and stayed to fight segregation. When Coles asked him why he risked his life to do this work, Dion said: "The satisfaction, man." Coles continued:

> When I asked him about those 'satisfactions,' he said, 'I'm meeting some really fine people. I'm listening to them tell me a lot about their lives. I'm hearing them stop and think about what they're willing to do to change this world here in Louisiana. Isn't that enough—isn't that a good reason to feel satisfied? If you can spend some of your life doing work like this, then you're lucky! There may be a sheriff out there waiting for me with a gun, but if he gets me, I'll die thinking: Dion, you actually *did* something—you were part of something much bigger than yourself, and you saw people beginning to change, right before your eyes, and that was a real achievement, and that's what I mean by 'satisfaction.'[2]

The Universal Importance of Service

The satisfaction that comes from service has been recognized throughout the world. Serving others is a fundamental, universal human value. It is emphasized in the teachings of the world's great religions, as well as statements by many respected thinkers and leaders.

Jesus said that he did not come to be served, but to serve. Paul, in his letter to the Galatians, told them to carry each other's burdens. In his first letter to the Corinthians, Paul said that nobody should seek his own good, but the good of others. St. Vincent de Paul said that the highest form of worship is service to humanity. John Wesley said: "Do all the good you can, by all the means you can, in all the ways you can, in all the places you can, at all the times you can, to all the people you can, as long as ever you can." Mother Teresa said: "There is joy in transcending self to serve others."

The Jewish Talmud says: "All men are responsible for one another." An Islamic text from the Hadith of Bukhari states that "the best of men are those who are useful to others." The Sufi Sheikh, M. R. Bawa Muhaiyaddeen, said: "To realize the pain and suffering of others and to offer your hands in assistance, helping to alleviate their suffering, is Islam."

The classic Taoist text, the *Tao Te Ching*, says that "the Way of Heaven is to benefit others and not to injure." The famous Hindu text, the *Bhagavad Gita*, states: "At the beginning, mankind and the obligation of selfless service were created together. 'Through selfless service, you will always be fruitful and find the fulfillment of your desires': this is the promise of the Creator ... He is present in every act of service."[3]

The Buddhist text, the *Shantideva* or Guide to the Bodhisattva's Way of Life, says: "If I employ others for my own purposes, I myself shall experience servitude. But if I use myself for the sake of others, I shall experience only lordliness."[4]

Among great thinkers, we can quote Aristotle, who said: "What is the essence of life? To serve others and do good." Cicero, the great Roman orator and philosopher, said: "Men were brought into existence for the sake of men that they might do one another good."

Albert Schweitzer said: "The purpose of human life is to serve and to show compassion and the will to help others." Martin Luther King, Jr. said: "Life's most persistent and urgent question is: What are you doing for others?" Rabindranath Tagore, the Nobel-Prize winning Indian poet, said: "I slept and dreamed that life was joy. I awoke and saw that life was service. I acted and behold, service was joy."

There is no question that for thousands of years, serving others has been highly valued by the world's great religions and many great thinkers.

Serving the Least Privileged

Robert Greenleaf was concerned about the effect that leadership has on the least privileged in society. Throughout the centuries, in diverse cultures around the world, special emphasis has been placed on serving those in greatest need. In the appendix of his book, *The Abolition of Man,* C. S. Lewis listed statements regarding moral practices that he called "The Tao or Natural Law." Here are some examples:

> Children, old men, the poor, and the sick, should be considered as lords of the atmosphere. (Hindu)

> In the Dalebura tribe a woman, a cripple from birth, was carried about by the tribes-people in turn until her death at the age of sixty-six... They never desert the sick. (Australian Aborigine)

> I tended the old man, I gave him my staff. (Ancient Egyptian)

> You will see them take care of widows, orphans, and old men, never reproaching them. (American Indian)

> Whoso makes intercession for the weak, well pleasing is this to Samas. (Babylonian)

> I have given bread to the hungry, water to the thirsty, clothes to the naked, a ferry boat to the boatless. (Ancient Egyptian)[5]

Jesus taught his followers to help "the least of these brothers of mine." In the parable of the sheep and the goats, found in Matthew 25, he urged his followers to feed the hungry, give drink to the thirsty, provide hospitality to strangers, clothe the naked, look after the sick, and visit those in prison.

Loving and helping others gives people a profound sense of meaning and purpose that can lead to deep happiness. One reason is that it is moral. In *The Call of Service*, Robert Coles said that "all service is directly or indirectly ethical activity, a reply to a moral call within, one that answers a moral need in the world."[6]

Several years ago, my wife and our three children and I spent Christmas vacation in Cambodia. Cambodia is one of the poorest countries in the world. From 1975 to 1979, when the Khmer Rouge were in power, an estimated two million Cambodians died. Many were tortured and killed for political reasons, but most died as a result of starvation, disease, and exhaustion from forced labor.

We were in Cambodia to visit Future Light Orphanage (FLO). Phaly Nuon, the founder and Executive Director of FLO, lived through the "killing fields." She was separated from her husband, and was forced to watch as her twelve-year-old daughter was raped by Khmer Rouge soldiers. Phaly fled into the jungle to hide with her three-year-old son and her newborn baby. As the months went by, she was unable to find food, and her baby died in her arms. She survived with her son, and began to work with other women who had lost their families. She and her husband founded a refugee camp to provide counseling for those suffering post traumatic distress. In 1993, they set up FLO as a non-governmental orphanage. It is located on her family's farm land on the outskirts of Phnom Penh. Phaly also founded the FLO-Khmer Silk Processing Association, a non-profit organization that produces silk products to provide jobs for widows and generate income for FLO.

FLO is more than an orphanage—it is a safe haven for children in a society that presses them toward begging, child labor, prostitution, and drugs. Many of the children who live at FLO have lost both parents, while some have a parent who is too poor to take care of them. FLO provides food, shelter, and clothing, including school uniforms and access to public education (which is not free). In addition, FLO teaches skills that can lead to good jobs. Tourism, technology, and textiles are promising industries, so children at FLO are taught English, traditional Cambodian dance, silk and wool weaving, and how to use computers.

Phaly began with the desire to serve, and emerged as a servant-leader who is having a profound impact on the lives of thousands of children. When I asked her how she became a leader, she seemed puzzled by the question. "Because the children needed help," she said simply.

Servant-leaders have a way of attracting other servant-leaders. We learned about Phaly and FLO from Rob Hail, a retired entrepreneur and full-time servant-leader. In the fall of 2000 Rob traveled through Vietnam, Thailand, and Cambodia visiting orphanages. He was impressed by the energy and vision of Phaly at FLO. He began lining up "e-mail foster parents" for individual children. Each foster parent agrees to donate money to support a child, and commits to sending and receiving e-mail messages with the foster child every month or two. Rob quickly lined up 75 foster parents, including my wife and me.

We fell in love with the children at FLO. We talked to them, and played with them, and on Christmas day, we dressed up as Santa and his helpers and handed out presents to each of them—all 240. On our last night at the orphanage, the children performed five traditional Cambodian dances for us, fully costumed, sharing their pride and considerable skill. There was such joy in their faces as they danced! We took pictures together, and dozens of the children brought us little gifts and notes they wanted us to take back to their foster parents. There were tears then, and again at the airport the next morning. We arrived with small material gifts, and departed with large spiritual ones. Serving others is like that.

Servant leadership starts with the desire to serve—a natural, moral desire that is recognized as important by the world's great religions and many great thinkers. Service makes a difference in the lives of both those who serve and those who are served. It builds relationships that offer meaning and hope.

2.

Who Is a Servant-Leader?

The idea of the leader as facilitator or servant is not new. In fact, it can be traced back thousands of years. For example, it can be found in the teachings of Lao-Tzu and Jesus.

Early Texts

One of the earliest recorded references to the leader as a facilitator instead of an autocratic ruler comes from a passage about leaders in the *Tao Te Ching*, attributed to Lao-Tzu, a sage who lived in China sometime between 570 B.C. and 490 B.C. Here is a translation of that passage by John C. H. Wu:

> The highest type of ruler is one of whose existence
>   the people are barely aware.
> Next comes one whom they love and praise.
> Next comes one whom they fear.
> Next comes one whom they despise and defy.
>
> When you are lacking in faith,
> Others will be unfaithful to you.
>
> The Sage is self-effacing and scanty of words.
> When his task is accomplished and things have been completed,
>   All the people say, 'We ourselves have achieved it!'[7]

An interpolation by Peter Merel concludes the same passage this way:

> When the best rulers achieve their purpose
> Their subjects claim the achievement as their own.

The best leaders are almost invisible. That is why, when great deeds are done, the people have a sense of ownership and accomplishment.

In his book *The Tao of Leadership: Lao Tzu's* Tao Te Ching *Adapted for a New Age,* John Heider explained the passage on leadership this way:

17. Being a Midwife

The wise leader does not intervene unnecessarily. The leader's presence is felt, but often the group runs itself. Lesser leaders do a lot, say a lot, have followers, and form cults. Even worse ones use fear to energize the group and force to overcome resistance ....

Remember that you are facilitating another person's process. It is not your process. Do not intrude. Do not control. Do not force your own needs and insights into the foreground. If you do not trust a person's process, that person will not trust you.

Imagine that you are a midwife; you are assisting at someone else's birth. Do good without show or fuss. Facilitate what is happening rather than what you think ought to be happening. If you must take the lead, lead so that the mother is helped, yet still free and in charge. When the baby is born, the mother will rightly say: 'We did it ourselves!'[8]

Early texts encouraged leaders to care for their followers. For example, in chapter 34 of the Old Testament book of Ezekiel, the Lord tells the prophet to say: "Woe to the shepherds of Israel who only take care of themselves! Should not shepherds take care of the flock?" This was echoed more than twelve hundred years later in an Islamic *hadith* in which Mohammed said to Muslim leaders: "Verily, each of you is a shepherd, and each of you is responsible for the well being of the flock."[9]

The earliest recorded statement specifically about servant leadership was made by Jesus, who contrasted servant leadership with power-oriented leadership. He gathered his disciples together and said to them:

"You know that the rulers of the Gentiles lord it over them, and their high officials exercise authority over them. Not so with you. Instead, whoever wants to become great among you must be your servant, and whoever wants to be first must be your slave—just as the Son of Man did not come to be served, but to serve, and to give his life as a ransom for many."[10]

On his last night with his disciples, Jesus got up from the table at which they had been eating, poured water into a basin, and washed the feet of his disciples. He told them that he did this to demonstrate how they were to serve each other.[11]

Defining the Servant-Leader

In Robert Greenleaf's seminal essay on *The Servant as Leader,* he defined the servant-leader this way:

> The servant-leader *is* servant first… It begins with the natural feeling that one wants to serve, to serve *first*. Then conscious choice brings one to aspire to lead. That person is sharply different from one who is *leader* first, perhaps because of the need to assuage an unusual power drive or to acquire material possessions .... The leader-first and the servant-first are two extreme types. Between them there are shadings and blends that are part of the infinite variety of human nature.
>
> The difference manifests itself in the care taken by the servant-first to make sure that other people's highest priority needs are being served. The best test, and difficult to administer, is: Do those served grow as persons? Do they, *while being served*, become healthier, wiser, freer, more autonomous, more likely themselves to become servants? *And,* what is the effect on the least privileged in society? Will they benefit or at least not be further deprived?[12]

In his second major essay, *The Institution as Servant,* Greenleaf shared his credo:

> This is my thesis: caring for persons, the more able and the less able serving each other, is the rock upon which a good society is built. Whereas, until recently, caring was largely person to person, now most of it is mediated through institutions—often large, complex, powerful, impersonal; not always competent; sometimes corrupt. If a better society is to be built, one that is more just and more loving, one that provides greater creative opportunity for its people, then the most open course is to *raise both the capacity to serve and the very performance as servant* of

existing major institutions by new regenerative forces operating within them.[13]

For Greenleaf, the goal was to make the world a better place. He called upon servant-leaders to transform their organizations into servant-institutions that will impact the world in positive ways.

So who, exactly, is a servant-leader? A servant-leader is simply *a leader who is focused on serving others.* A servant-leader loves people and wants to help them. The mission of the servant-leader is therefore to identify and meet the needs of others. Loving and helping others gives a servant-leader meaning and satisfaction in life.

Servant-leaders can be government officials, business executives, academic administrators, non-profit leaders, military commanders, coaches, friends, or neighbors. Servant-leaders do most of the things that other leaders do—they articulate a vision, they manage, they communicate, and so forth. What sets servant-leaders apart from other leaders is their desire to serve. As a result, they are focused on others, not just themselves, and they are motivated to make life better for others, not just for themselves. This difference in focus and motivation is what really distinguishes servant-leaders, regardless of their titles, roles, or positions.

What are the characteristics of a servant-leader? In his essay *The Servant as Leader,* Greenleaf made it clear that the most important characteristic was the desire to serve. He also emphasized listening and understanding; acceptance and empathy; foresight; awareness; persuasion; conceptualization; self-healing; and rebuilding community. He said that servant-leaders initiate action, are goal-oriented, are dreamers of great dreams, are good communicators, are able to withdraw and re-orient themselves, and are dependable, trusted, creative, intuitive, and situational.

Larry Spears identified ten characteristics of the servant-leader: listening, empathy, healing, awareness, persuasion, conceptualization, foresight, stewardship, commitment to the growth of people, and building community.[14]

Bill Turner, former Chairman and CEO of W.C. Bradley Company and Synovus Financial, developed his own list of the common qualities of servant-leaders. Those qualities are unconditional love, brokenness, self-awareness, being real, foresight, facilitating a common vision, building community, empowering others, meeting the needs of others and removing obstacles, and being a cheerleader.[15]

The Center for Servant Leadership at the Pastoral Institute in Columbus, Georgia, describes servant leadership as a lifelong journey that includes discovery of one's self, a desire to serve others, and a commitment to lead. The servant-leader is someone who continuously strives to be trustworthy, self-aware, humble, caring, visionary, empowering, relational, competent, a good steward, and a community builder.

Scholars are identifying characteristics of servant leadership in order to develop and test theories about the impact of servant leadership. For example, Robert C. Liden and his colleagues identified nine dimensions of servant leadership that they used in their research: emotional healing, creating value for the community, conceptual skills, empowering, helping subordinates grow and succeed, putting subordinates first, behaving ethically, relationships, and servanthood.[16] Dirk van Dierendonck reviewed the scholarly literature and identified six key characteristics of servant-leader behavior: empowering and developing people, humility, authenticity, interpersonal acceptance, providing direction, and stewardship.[17]

Whatever their qualities or characteristics, servant-leaders have a desire to serve. Some start out that way, early in life. Others start out with a desire for power, wealth, and fame, and then discover that there is more joy in serving others. Leadership becomes meaningful when it is a way of helping others.

Examples of Servant-Leaders in History

There are no doubt thousands of examples of servant-leaders in history, literature, the movies, and daily life today. One thinks of historical figures like George Washington, Abraham Lincoln, Florence Nightingale, Susan B. Anthony, Albert Schweitzer, Gandhi, Martin Luther King, Jr., Nelson Mandela, Cesar Chavez, and Mother Teresa. Three of my favorites are

George Williams, Harriet Tubman, and Eiichi Shibusawa.

George Williams was a young man who worked in a draper's shop in London in 1844. He was a sales assistant, and like lots of other young men in London at the time, he worked ten to twelve hours a day, six days a week. At night, he slept in a crowded room over his workplace. Williams noticed that young men like himself had few positive alternatives to life on the streets. So he gathered together a group of other drapers, and they formed a Christian fellowship of young men who were committed to helping each other grow in mind and spirit. That group became the YMCA, which today serves forty-five million men, women, and children through hundreds of programs in 124 countries.

Harriet Tubman was born into slavery in 1822. As a teenage field hand, she was nearly killed when hit in the head by an iron weight thrown by an overseer at a fleeing slave. That injury plagued her for the rest of her life. When her owner died in 1849, she traveled the Underground Railroad to freedom in Philadelphia. The Underground Railroad was a secret series of houses, tunnels, and roads set up by abolitionists and former slaves to provide an escape route for slaves. From 1850 to 1860, Tubman traveled to the South about eighteen times, and helped three hundred slaves escape to freedom, including her brothers and parents. She settled many of them in Canada, where they could not be recaptured. Southerners tried to put a stop to her work by putting out rewards for her capture. She was reverently called "Moses" by the slaves she helped to freedom.

During the Civil War, Tubman provided nursing care for black soldiers and newly freed slaves in Union camps. She spied and scouted behind Confederate lines, and even led a military raid on a Confederate outpost, freeing 700 slaves. After the war, she became a community activist and campaigned for women's rights. Toward the end of her life, she established a home for the aged on land next to her own house in Auburn, New York. Tubman was a servant-leader, fighting for the freedom and rights of others.

Eiichi Shibusawa was a Japanese industrialist who lived from 1840 to 1931. Shibusawa was born into the peasant class. At the age of twenty-seven he visited Europe, and came to understand the importance of industrial and economic development. When the Meiji Restoration began, he became a member of the elite Ministry of Finance. He left the ministry to become president of Japan's first modern bank. Using the bank as his base, he began building the economy of Japan by establishing businesses of all kinds. During his lifetime he founded and developed more than six hundred industrial companies, creating tens of thousands of jobs.

Shibusawa's focus was on maximizing talent—developing human capital. He believed that good ethics and business should go together. He served as an unofficial management counselor, helping hundreds of civil servants, businessmen, and managers. He also organized training programs, supported higher education for women, and engaged in projects to promote social welfare. One of his legacies was the establishment of a famous university of economics. Shibusawa was a servant-leader, focused on building his nation by creating opportunities for his fellow countrymen.

Servant-Leaders in Our Communities

While there have been many famous servant-leaders, most servant-leaders have not been known outside the group or community they have served. They did not seek fame, they sought to make a difference—and they did.

Servant-leaders are active throughout the world in the Rotary movement, where "Service Above Self" has long been a cherished motto. Founded in 1905, Rotary has approximately 1.2 million members working in 34,000 clubs in more than two hundred countries and geographical areas. Rotary International launched a polio eradication program in 1988, when polio was common throughout the world. Since then, Rotarians and their partner agencies have immunized more than two billion children in 122 countries, reducing polio from 350,000 cases in 1988 to fewer than 650 cases in 2011—a 99.8 percent reduction. It is estimated that four million children who might have contracted polio have been saved from the crippling disease. Rotarians raised more than $1 billion, and tens of thousands of Rotarians have assisted in distributing the polio vaccine.

Individuals make a difference. For example, Will Hartzell is a friend of mine who learned that each year contaminated drinking water causes the deaths of millions of people around the world. He made a deep personal commitment to change that. He developed solar water pasteurizers that are a simple, low-cost, long-term solution to the problem. In spite of all the "naysayers" who told him it couldn't be done, he launched his company, Safe Water Systems, in 1996. Will recalled:

> One safe-drinking-water project that left an indelible impact on me was in Africa. Our Solar Water Pasteurizers were installed in five locations near Arusha, Tanzania. One site was the Selian Hospital. The hospital was not able to afford a water disinfection system and ran the risk of patients actually contracting diseases while at the hospital.
>
> After our equipment was installed, I was watching the patients as they came to get clean water to drink. One woman was in the hospital because her child was gravely ill. After she filled her water bottle and was headed back to her child, she stopped and looked at me. Our eyes met in one of those time-stopping moments. We didn't speak the same language, but the nurse translated for me. She said, "Thank you. Thank you for giving my child the chance to live."
>
> At that moment I knew that I would do whatever it took to provide safe drinking water for as many people as I could all over the world.[18]

Since then, Will and his colleagues have installed 4,000 solar water pasteurizers and other water purification systems in fifty-three countries. The result is that 400,000 people in those countries no longer risk illness or death because of contaminated water. Will Hartzell is a servant-leader who saves lives every day.

After the racial riots in Detroit in 1967, Eleanor Josaitis and her friend and pastor Father William Cunningham decided to do something. Father Cunningham left his teaching job at a seminary and began working at a parish in the inner city. Eleanor and her husband sold their suburban home and moved their family to a neighborhood where rioting had occurred. Together, Josaitis and Cunningham founded an organization they called Focus: HOPE that is dedicated to providing practical solutions to racism and poverty.

During the next thirty years, they built an organization that provides food for women and children; fights discriminatory grocery prices in low-income neighborhoods; operates a Montessori preschool for students and community members; creates employment opportunities through a Machinist Training Institute; runs a FAST TRACK program to help students improve their reading and math skills so they can enter training programs; and offers a First Step program in reading and math to help students qualify for FAST TRACK.

By 2007, Focus: HOPE had trained more than 2,700 qualified machinists and graduated nearly 6,000 people from First Step and FAST TRACK. Their Center for Advanced Technologies graduated more than one hundred manufacturing engineers with associate or bachelor degrees granted by cooperating universities, and their Information Technology Center had graduated nearly six hundred students. And Focus: HOPE was feeding 43,000 low-income elderly, mothers, and children each month.[19] Cunningham and Josaitis demonstrated how servant-leaders can transform neighborhoods and create opportunities that change the lives of thousands of people.

Takeshi Oishi was an educator, serving forty years as a teacher and principal of an elementary school in Japan. Toward the end of his career, he became a member of a government committee that studied social issues. During that time, he learned about the plight of the mentally challenged and their need for specially designed housing and training.

When Mr. Oishi retired, he looked for land that could be used to build a home for mentally challenged individuals. He not only found an appropriate site—he convinced the owner to donate the land. It took years to negotiate the permits and approvals, raise the money, and complete construction, but the new center was finally built. When Mr. Oishi died in 1995, all fifty of the residents of the center attended his funeral, sitting in the front row to pay their respects to the man who had given them a home. Takeshi Oishi was a servant-leader who identified and met the special needs of others.

Servant-Leaders in Fiction

Robert Greenleaf's concept of the servant-leader was stimulated by his reading of *Journey to the East* by Herman Hesse. It is the story of a group of travelers who were served by Leo, who did their menial chores and lifted them with his spirit and his song. All went well until Leo disappeared one day. The travelers fell into disarray and could go no farther on their own. The journey was over. Years later, one of the travelers saw Leo again—as the revered head of the Order that sponsored the journey. Leo, who was their servant, was the titular head of the Order, a great and noble leader. Greenleaf observed that "this story clearly says that *the great leader is seen as servant first,* and that simple fact is the key to his greatness. Leo was actually the leader all of the time, but he was servant first because that was what he was, *deep down inside.*"[20]

One of my favorite servant-leaders in fiction is Atticus Finch, the father and attorney in *To Kill a Mockingbird,* the Pulitzer-Prize winning novel by Harper Lee. The story is set in a small southern town during the depression of the 1930s. Atticus Finch, portrayed in the movie by Gregory Peck, is a lawyer who defended a black man, Tom Robinson, who was unjustly accused of raping a white girl. In a time of racial passions, the jury ignored the obvious facts. Atticus lost the trial, and Tom, who was certain that there was no hope in appealing his conviction, was shot when he tried to escape.

Although Atticus lost the trial, what was important is that he placed himself in service to another, and at great personal risk, stood for what was right. Those around him respected his quiet courage. Immediately after the jury issued its guilty verdict, Atticus said some reassuring words to Tom, chatted briefly with the court reporter, and then began packing up his books and papers. Members of the black community, who were sitting in the balcony, watched him packing up. One by one, they stood up, in a silent gesture of respect. His daughter was in the balcony with them, and as Atticus turned to leave the courtroom, Reverend Sykes leaned over and said to her: "Miss Jean Louise! Miss Jean Louise! Stand up. Your father's passing!"

In fantasy novels, there are wizards who are servant-leaders, such as Gandalf in *The Lord of the Rings* by J. R. R. Tolkien, Belgarath in *The Belgariad* by David Eddings, and Ged in *The Earthsea Trilogy* by Ursula Le Guin. Each wizard provides wisdom and guidance, and makes sacrifices for the good of the group.

Another great example of a servant-leader is Hazel-rah, the Chief

Rabbit in the novel *Watership Down* by Richard Adams. This is a wonderful fable about a group of rabbits who set out to find a new home. Hazel-rah becomes the Chief Rabbit, not because he is the biggest rabbit in the group, or the most clever, or the most clairvoyant. He becomes the leader because he is willing to listen, and he often asks for advice from others. He knows the different strengths of the other rabbits, and draws out those strengths for the good of the group. He is able to identify the needs of the group, and make decisions and take action in a way that unites the rabbits in seeking to achieve their common goals. And he is willing to pitch in and take personal risks on behalf of the group. The rabbits face hard times, and are severely tested, but with Hazel-rah's guidance, they work together as a team, and they succeed in finding a new home.

One of the many movies made by Kurosawa Akira is titled *Ikiru*, which means "to live" in Japanese. It is the story of Kanji Watanabe, a Japanese government bureaucrat who discovered that he was dying of cancer and had only six months to live. After wandering around the city feeling sorry for himself, he decided to make a difference before he died.

Watanabe set out to establish a playground for a neighborhood whose children had no place to play. The mothers of the neighborhood had approached the government and asked that a playground be built, but they had been referred from government agency to government agency, each bureaucrat passing the buck to the other. Nobody was willing to take responsibility and help them. Watanabe, a branch chief in the Citizen's Section, decided to take up their cause. While enduring great physical pain, he patiently and courageously confronted each obstacle until he got the playground built. He died late one night, sitting in one of the swings in the playground, softly singing one of his favorite songs, completely at peace with himself. At last his life meant something. He had helped somebody. He had become a servant-leader, and he had made a difference.

3.

Power Model vs. Service Model

In his definition of the servant-leader, Greenleaf distinguished between the servant-first and the leader-first. The servant-first lives the *service* model of leadership. The leader-first lives the *power* model of leadership.[21] The power model is *neither* moral nor effective, while the service model is *both* moral and effective.

According to the power model, leadership is about how to accumulate and wield power, how to make people do things, how to attack and win. It is about clever strategies, applying pressure, and manipulating people to get what you want. A word that is often used is *realpolitik*. It means politics and the exercise of power with no reference to morality or ethics.

Problems with the Power Model

There are some severe problems with the power model. First, the power model focuses on *having* power, not on using it wisely. Power is an end in itself. This leads to the second problem, which is that the power model defines success or victory in terms of *who gains more power,* not in terms of who accomplishes the most for his or her organization or community. Factions may brilliantly battle other factions, and great victories and defeats may occur between them, with no benefit to the organization or society at large. In fact, rather than healing and building, factional warfare between rival power groups usually results in more hurt and more fragmentation.

A third problem with the power model of leadership is that it promotes conflict between power groups. A person wants to be a leader, and since he has been told that leadership is about power, he builds his power base. But then, other would-be leaders are building their power bases, too. Pretty soon, leaders in the power model are so focused on fighting rival power factions, that they have little time to focus on problems that need to be solved or opportunities that need to be seized. And without that focus, organizations and communities don't move forward. The problems continue, and the dreams go unfulfilled.

Other problems with the power model relate to the leader herself or himself. People who seek power often become irrelevant as leaders. They focus on what *they* want, instead of what other people want, and they lose touch with the people they are supposed to be serving. Of course, they may remain in power because they are good at maintaining their power base, but even then, they may never be happy. That's because people who seek power can never get enough of it. Power becomes a kind of addiction or disease. They always want more, and more, and more. This easily results in spiritual corruption and an unhappy life of self-torment.

An example from literature is Shakespeare's *Macbeth*, a tragedy set in medieval Scotland. Macbeth is a loyal and courageous Scottish general who defeats an invading army. He encounters a group of witches who prophesy that he will be thane of Cawdor and eventually king, while the heirs of another Scottish general, Banquo, will also become kings in their day.

Then Macbeth learns that as a reward for his victory, King Duncan has just made him the thane of Cawdor. With the first part of the prophesy fulfilled, Macbeth's ambition becomes so strong that he abandons all moral constraints. Encouraged by his wife, he murders King Duncan, and then, as a cover-up, blames and murders two chamberlains. He also hires murderers to kill Banquo, and after receiving further prophesies from the witches, he orders the murders of the wife and children of Macduff, a Scottish nobleman who opposes him. Macbeth becomes a tyrant, feared by all. Lady Macbeth, haunted by all the bloodshed, goes insane and finally commits suicide. Duncan's son raises an army in England, and with the support of other Scottish nobles, the army defeats Macbeth, who is killed by Macduff in combat.

The central theme is that Macbeth wanted power, and his ambition corrupted him. He abandoned his loyalty and morality, and became a murderer. But becoming the king wasn't enough for him. Macbeth became paranoid. He knew that there were others who could take his power from him. He didn't want to give up his power, so he continued killing. Power was addictive, and he could never be at peace.

A modern literary example was provided by Robert Penn Warren, who won a Pulitzer Prize for his brilliant novel, *All the King's Men*. The novel is about the transformation of Willie Stark from a country lawyer with good intentions to a power-hungry politician. He began by fighting the corrupt political machine. He got elected governor, and did good things for the people. But his desire for power gradually swallowed his desire to serve, and he became the head of his own corrupt political machine. It is a brooding, unsettling story of a man who set out to serve others, and ended by making them serve him.

Sometimes, people think they are serving others, but are really using the power model instead. In his essay on *The Servant as Leader*, Greenleaf mentioned Ken Kesey's book, *One Flew Over the Cuckoo's Nest*. Greenleaf noted that the nurse in the novel was strong, able, dedicated, dominating, authority-ridden, manipulative, and exploitative. The net effect of her influence "diminished other people, literally destroyed them."[22] She did battle with MacMurphy, a patient who helped others to become healthier and stronger. We feel the pain and loss when the nurse wins, and MacMurphy dies.

Machiavelli and the Amoral Use of Power

Perhaps the most famous intellectual to argue for the amoral use of raw power was Niccolo Machiavelli, who lived in Florence in the fifteenth century. According to scholar Max Lerner, Machiavell's book *The Prince* is "one of the half dozen books that have done most to shape Western thought."[23] Perhaps that is why the power model is so dominant in our culture.

Lerner said that Machiavelli rejected theology and idealism in favor of "political realism." He abandoned what was ethical in favor of what was "realistic." For example, in *The Prince*, Machiavelli argued that "in taking a state the conqueror must arrange to commit all his cruelties at once, so as not to have to recur to them every day."[24] He said that since so many people are not good, "it is necessary for a prince, who wishes to maintain himself, to learn how not to be good ..."[25] He urged that "a prudent ruler ought not to keep faith when by so doing it would be against his interest, and when the reasons which made him bind himself no longer exist."[26] Since it looks good when a leader overcomes difficulties, "a wise prince ought, when he has the chance, to foment astutely some enmity, so that by suppressing it he will augment his greatness."[27]

Most of us are fascinated by power, and many of us want to have some. We may be tempted by the "realistic" approach that advises the use of raw power, an approach that is especially easy to find in the works of military and political strategists. A recent example is Robert Greene's book, *The 48 Laws of Power*. The book jacket, which is designed to sell the book, says:

> The bestselling book for those who want POWER, watch POWER, or want to arm themselves against POWER. Amoral, cunning, ruthless, and instructive, this piercing work distills three thousand years of the history of power into forty-eight well-explicated laws ... synthesizing the philosophies of Machiavelli, Sun-tzu, Carl von Clausewitz, and other great thinkers.

Greene said in his Preface:

> The feeling of having no power over people and events is generally unbearable to us—when we feel helpless we feel miserable. No one wants less power; everyone wants more. In the world today, however, it is dangerous to seem too power hungry, to be overt with your power moves. We have to seem fair and decent. So we need to be subtle—congenial yet cunning, democratic yet devious.[28]

The so-called "laws of power" that are described in Greene's book are based on deceit, cunning, treachery, and conquest, all for personal gain. They are about hiding your intentions, grabbing the credit, keeping people dangling, being selectively honest, pretending to be a friend while being a spy, and exploiting people's need to believe. Should we wonder why the world is the way that it is, when the power model is the dominant model of leadership?

Morality is about right and wrong behavior. The power model is not really concerned with that—it is concerned with acquiring and wielding power. If pretending to care about people is good for acquiring power, the power-seeking leader will pretend to care. The leader will identify some needs, and will make promises about meeting those needs. But once in power, the leader may do little to implement those promises. In fact the leader is likely to do just enough, and *only* just enough, to keep his or her power. Even worse, a leader may make caring statements, and then do the opposite.

If a leader who lives the power model can gain power without helping anybody, he or she will do so. In fact, the leader may feel justified in making life *worse* for a lot of people, so long as he or she gains power. Power is self-justifying; power itself is the end. It is not a means to make life better for others, except the power holders and their close friends. That is why *leaders who live the power model are not very effective in meeting human needs or making life better for others. It's not what they are trying to do.* It's not their focus. It's not what they care about. Often, they can gain and maintain power while being remarkably indifferent to the needs of others.

Servant Leadership Has a Moral Base

Unlike the power model, the service model does have a moral base. The whole point of the service model is to be of service—to identify and meet the needs of others. It is about paying attention to others and treating them right.

To accept the reality of pain and suffering in the world, and only exploit it for private gain, is morally wrong and ignores all the higher aspirations of human beings since time immemorial—aspirations found in moral and ethical codes, as well as religious and spiritual teachings. These aspirations are made all the more urgent by the daily cries for help of those who are disadvantaged. The power model perpetuates fear, war, violence, disease, and starvation. If people continue to use the power model, we will make little progress in bringing peace or justice to the world.

Machiavelli and Greene say: This is the way the world is—turn it to your personal advantage. We need to hear a different voice, a voice that says: Here is the way the world *could* be—let's turn it to *everyone's* advantage.

Greenleaf said that "caring for persons, the more able and the less able serving each other, is the rock upon which a good society is built."[29] And that is what servant-leaders do, by living the service model of leadership. The servant-leader does not ask, "How can I get power? How can I make people do things?" The servant-leader asks, "What do people need? How can I help them to get it? What does my organization need to do? How can I help my organization to do it?" Thus, rather than embarking on a quest for personal power, the servant-leader embarks on a quest to identify and meet the needs of others. It is this daily quest that results in improving organizations and the lives of the people they serve; it is this daily quest that lifts communities and societies for the benefit of all.

For Servant-Leaders Power Is Only a Tool

Of course, we live in a real world. We know that power abhors a vacuum. Somebody is going to exercise power, and it makes a difference who that somebody is. Certainly, a servant-leader can accumulate and exercise power. A servant-leader can even become angry and enter the fray to do battle. What is important is that the servant-leader accumulates power or becomes angry *on behalf of others.* A servant-leader acts in response to the way *others* are treated, not in response to the way he or she is treated. The servant-leader knows that power is a means, not an end. It is only a tool. Often, it is not even the most important tool. There are many tools, such as listening and coaching, that turn out to be more important than power.

Because power is only a tool, great servant-leaders have been willing to give it up when they no longer need it to serve others. Cincinnatus, George Washington, and Jose de San Martin are good examples. They made the leadership contribution that was needed at the time, and then passed the power to others.

Cincinnatus was a Roman political leader and general who lived in the fifth century B.C. He is a semi-legendary figure often cited as a model of Roman virtue. He lived a simple life, working on his own farm. He served as a Roman consul in 460 B.C. When the Aequi tribe and the Volscians threatened Rome in 458 B.C., the Senate begged Cincinnatus to become the absolute dictator and save Rome. Cincinnatus was reluctant to become the absolute dictator, because he was needed on the farm. If his crops weren't sown in a timely manner, his family could starve. But he agreed to serve. Organizing the troops, he defeated the Aequi and Volscians in sixteen days. He then resigned his absolute authority, and returned to farming. He came out of retirement to do the same thing again, twenty years later.

George Washington is sometimes described as a modern Cincinnatus. Washington was a surveyor and a farmer, widely respected as a person of good character who was focused on public service. He was the general of the Continental Army, president of the Constitutional Convention, and the first president of the United States. He was so admired that if he had wanted to be king, the United States might have become a constitutional monarchy. But that is not what Washington wanted. He didn't want to be king, he wanted to be a public servant. He voluntarily resigned his commission as general after the war, and later, after two terms as president, he decided not to run again, giving the nation a successful transition of power. Historian Joseph Ellis said that Washington was "the supreme example of the leader who could be trusted with power because he was so ready to give it up."[30]

Jose de San Martin is another famous leader who twice gave up his power. Born in 1778 in what is now Argentina, San Martin received a military education in Spain and served in the Spanish Army. In 1812 he returned to Argentina to join the rebels who were fighting to free South America from Spanish rule. Although Argentina was declared independent in 1816, San Martin knew that Argentina would not remain independent if the Spanish still controlled Chile and Peru. In 1817 he joined Chilean leader Bernardo O'Higgins and led an army of 5,000 men on a dangerous march through the snowy Andes mountains to Chile, where they defeated the Spanish. Chile was declared independent in 1818. San Martin declined to be the Chilean president, giving that honor to O'Higgins instead.

San Martin next assembled a fleet and sailed north to attack the Spanish at Peru. In 1821 he declared Peru an independent nation, and was named the governor. When his vision of how to organize the newly independent countries of South America came in conflict with another patriot, Simon Bolivar, who had been fighting further north, San Martin deferred to Bolivar, returned to Argentina, and eventually retired in Europe. Many Argentineans consider San Martin their greatest national hero. He fought for others, not himself, and he gave up his power to others, rather than keeping it for himself.

Power as a Gift

The paradox is that a servant-leader can gain power without seeking it. People trust servant-leaders, and give them power, because they know that servant-leaders use power to benefit everyone. James Autry wrote:

> ... [T]rue power comes from the people. It comes from gaining the trust and support of the people who then give you the power. Power is like love. The more you try to give it to others, the more it just seems to flow to you naturally.[31]

Power is given to a servant-leader as a gift, by others who trust the leader. So long as the servant-leader continues to serve others well, there is no reason for anyone to take back their gift of power.

On the other hand, when a leader grabs power, the leader will constantly have to fight to keep it. If the leader had to grab it, it means that others don't want the leader to have it, or they want it for themselves instead. The leader will constantly be defending his turf. After all, if the leader grabbed power, somebody else can grab it back, just because *they* want it. So the leader has to keep fighting rivals, and building ever-shifting alliances, and trying to be the power broker, and trying to defeat the plans of others so they will not get credit for accomplishing things that might in turn enhance their power and threaten the leader. The leader ends up being so busy defending his turf, that he really doesn't have time to do much else.

People Want to Follow Servant-Leaders

When servant-leaders work on problems and opportunities, they don't carry a lot of ego baggage. They don't worry about their own personal status or prestige. They just focus on the problem or opportunity. That makes it a lot easier for people to work with them and follow them. It makes it easier to build teams and partnerships and get things done. There's an old saying, "it's amazing how much we get done around here when nobody cares who gets the credit." That's what servant-leaders are like. They are focused on the work, not the credit.

Servant-leaders are human and make mistakes. However, people are willing to follow servant-leaders because they know that servant-leaders are not in it for themselves. As Greenleaf wrote in his essay, *The Servant as Leader:*

> A fresh critical look is being taken at the issues of power and authority, and people are beginning to learn, however haltingly, to relate to one another in less coercive and more creatively supporting ways. A new moral principle is emerging which holds that the only authority deserving one's allegiance is that which is freely and knowingly granted by the led to the leader in response to, and in proportion to, the clearly evident servant stature of the leader. Those who choose to follow this principle will not casually accept the authority of existing institutions. *Rather, they will freely respond only to individuals who are chosen as leaders because they are proven and trusted as servants.* To the extent that this principle prevails in the future, the only truly viable institutions will be those that are predominantly servant-led.[32]

A servant-leader is by far the best leader to take an organization through a period of change. The reason is that a servant-leader will not use organizational change as the excuse for building his or her own power and position. The servant-leader will not make changes based on personalities, factional politics, and competition between rivals. The servant-leader will be focused instead on meeting the needs of the organization and those it serves. The servant-leader will be listening, consulting, and analyzing information so that the organization can adapt and remain relevant to changing needs. Hard decisions may have to be made, but if so, they will be made by giving priority to the needs of others.

The Unifying Dream

Servant-leaders know that it is not about them, it is about making a difference. Often, they are able to unite their colleagues through the development of a shared dream or vision of a better future. In his essay, *The Leadership Crisis*, Greenleaf said:

> ... Institutions function better when the idea, the dream, is to the fore, and the person, the leader, is seen as the servant of the idea. It is not 'I,' the ultimate leader, that is moving this institution to greatness; it is the dream, the great idea. 'I' am subordinate to the idea; 'I' am servant of the idea along with everyone else who is involved in the effort .... The leader leads well when leadership is, and is seen as, serving the dream and searching for a better one .... It is the *idea* that unites people in the common effort, not the charisma of the leader. It is the communicated faith of the leader in the dream that enlists dedicated support needed to move people toward accomplishment of the dream.[33]

Servant-leaders help their colleagues to develop, articulate, and work toward a dream that is inspiring and truly meets the needs of others.

Service, Love, and Community

Greenleaf pointed out that serving each other requires love. He noted that love is undefinable. "But it begins, I believe, with one absolute condition: unlimited liability! As soon as one's liability for another is qualified to any degree, love is diminished by that much."[34] Greenleaf went on to say that "any human service where the one who is served should be loved in the process requires community, a face-to-face group in which the liability of each for the other and all for one is unlimited, or as close to it as it is possible to get."[35]

Bill Turner emphasized the importance of building a community as part of his journey in building successful companies like Synovus Financial, which *Fortune* magazine rated the #1 Best Company to Work for in America in 1999. In his book, *The Learning of Love: A Journey Toward Servant Leadership*, Turner said:

> Servant leadership must be grounded in a love that is a spiritual gift. And it must reach outside the organization in many ways to create a caring community and ultimately to build a better world. In a servant-

led organization, the basis for all decision making should be, 'What is the loving thing to do?'

There is a deep spiritual hunger in all of us to find a place where people really care for one another, where we can find something to believe in and something and someone to trust. When these things are discovered together in community, great things can happen. Believing in the worth and goodness of people is basic to servant leadership.[36]

Juana Bordas, in her book *Salsa, Soul and Spirit*, points out that "servant leadership is deeply anchored in Black, American Indian, and Latino cultures that center on community responsibility, the public welfare, and addressing the social structures that hinder people's progress."[37] These ethnic groups have defined leadership as community servanthood— serving the collective. "Leaders, therefore, are like good stewards who build community capacity and group empowerment."[38] Because the leaders understand that their first responsibility is to promote the good of the entire community, people trust their leaders and are willing to place the community in their hands.

Bordas said that "leaders grow their communities by engaging people in the following practices: (1) encouraging participation and building consensus, (2) creating a community of leaders, (3) generating a shared vision, (4) using culturally effective communication, and (5) weaving partnerships and connections."[39] The "top" leadership positions are often rotated among individuals, because leadership does not belong to a person, it belongs to the community. Leaders set high standards and follow the same rules as other community members. It is expected that leaders will not take more than their fair share of community resources. Leadership is not about the power of an individual, but rather, the good of all.

This focus on building and serving the larger community is a key difference between the power model and the service model of leadership. In her talk on "The Work of the Servant-Leader," Margaret Wheatley said:

> There are many patterns, many beliefs, out there about leadership, about people, about motivation, about human development. The essential truth I'm discovering right now is that when we are together, more becomes possible. When we are together, joy is available. In the

midst of a world that is insane, that will continue to surprise us with new outrages ... in the midst of that future, the gift is each other. We have lived with a belief system that has not told us that. We have lived with a belief that has said, 'We're in it for ourselves. It's a dog-eat-dog world out there. Only the strong survive and you can't trust anybody.' That's the belief that's operating in most organizations if you scratch the surface. The belief that called you to be a servant-leader, I believe, is the belief of who we are as a species. We have need for each other. We have a desire for each other, and, more and more, I believe that if the *real work is to stay together*, then we are not only the best resource to move into this future—we are the only resource .... We need to learn how to be together: that is the essential work of the servant-leader.[40]

Simple Ways to Contrast the Power and Service Models

There are some simple ways to contrast a power-oriented leader and a service-oriented leader. The first is this: Power-oriented leaders want to *make* people do things. Servant-leaders want to *help* people do things. That's why servant-leaders are usually facilitators, coordinators, healers, partners, and coalition-builders.

Another way to contrast the two models is this. The power model assumes a hierarchy shaped like a pyramid. Only a few people have power—those at the top of the pyramid—so it is assumed that only they can be leaders. In the service model, the hierarchy doesn't matter. That's because *anybody* in a family, organization, or community can be of service. *Anybody* can identify and meet the needs of others. *Anybody* can be a servant-leader.

At bottom, the difference between the two models is simple. The power model is about *grabbing*. The service model is about *giving*.

We have to decide. Are we going to grab, or give? Are we going to *use* people, or *help* people? It's a fundamental moral decision. Albert Einstein said: "The high destiny of the individual is to serve rather than to rule." Servant leadership is a way to work toward that high destiny.

4.

The Key Practices
of Servant-Leaders

Servant leadership is not only a moral approach to leadership, it is also the most effective way of leading. Servant leadership really *works*, and it works in all types of organizations, in all sectors—public, private, non-profit, and academic.

Robert Greenleaf worked for AT&T when it was one of the largest corporations in the world. His final role there was Director of Management Research. He continually sought ways to improve the leadership and management of the company. After retiring from AT&T, he reflected, and concluded that the best approach to leadership is servant leadership. Many experts agree.

What the Experts Say

Ken Blanchard met Robert Greenleaf in the late 1960s when Blanchard was at Ohio University and Greenleaf came to spend a weekend with the students. Blanchard is convinced that servant leadership is the foundation for effective leadership. He said:

> I truly believe that servant leadership has never been more applicable to the world of leadership than it is today. Not only are people looking for a deeper purpose and meaning when they must meet the challenges of today's changing world; they are also looking for principles and philosophies that actually work. Servant leadership works. Servant leadership is about getting people to a higher level by leading people at a higher level.[41]

In *Leading at a Higher Level*, Blanchard said: "Servant leadership is not just another management technique. It is a way of life for those with servant hearts."[42] Blanchard argued that servant leadership provides better leadership because the vision and values are established up front, and servant leadership requires the kind of humility that brings out the best in both the leaders and those they serve. Servant leadership also results in better service, because frontline people are encouraged and empowered to develop strong relationships with customers. Servant leadership creates high performing organizations, because it supports shared power and high involvement throughout the organization. Servant-leaders capitalize on diversity in cultures, styles, social relationships, race, religion, sexual orientation, and age. They know that when people—all their people—are involved in decisions that affect their lives, they are healthier, happier, feel less stress, and have a greater sense of ownership and commitment. Finally, organizations led by servant-leaders are more likely to generate both success and significance—both bottom line results and the meaning that comes from generosity, service, and loving relationships.[43]

Stephen Covey is also a champion of servant leadership. He said:

> The deepest part of human nature is that which urges people— each one of us—to rise above our present circumstances and to transcend our nature. If you can appeal to it, you tap into a whole new source of human motivation. Perhaps that is why I have found Robert Greenleaf's teaching on servant leadership to be so enormously inspiring, so uplifting, so ennobling.
>
> A great movement is taking place throughout the world today. Its roots, I believe, are to be found in two powerful forces. One is the dramatic globalization of markets and technology. And in a very pragmatic way, this tidal wave of change is fueling the impact of the second force: timeless, universal principles that have governed, and always will govern, all enduring success, especially those principles that give 'air' and 'life' and creative power to the human spirit that *produces* value in markets, organizations, families, and, most significantly, individual's lives.
>
> One of these fundamental, timeless principles is the idea of servant leadership, and I am convinced that it will continue to dramatically increase in its relevance ...[44]

Experts in business leadership and management often describe the effective leader as a servant-leader without using the words "servant-leader." For example, Peter Drucker, in his book *The Effective Executive*, said that the key question that distinguishes an executive is the question: "What can I contribute?" Drucker said:

> The effective executive focuses on contribution .... He asks: 'What can I contribute that will significantly affect the performance and the results of the institution I serve?' .... The focus on contribution turns the executive's attention away from his own specialty, his own narrow skills, his own department, and toward the performance of the whole ... to the entire organization and its purpose. He therefore will also come to think in terms of the customer, the client, or the patient, who is the ultimate reason for whatever the organization produces ...[45]

Drucker described the effective executive as someone who is focused on contribution and focused on others—a good definition of servant leadership in business.

Peter M. Senge is the author of *The Fifth Discipline* and a founder of the Society for Organizational Learning. In a talk published in *Reflections on Leadership*, he said:

> I believe that the book Servant Leadership, and in particular the essay, "The Servant as Leader," which starts the book off, is the most singular and useful statement on leadership that I have read in the last 20 years. Despite the virtual tidal wave of books on leadership during the last few years, there is something different about Bob Greenleaf's essay, something both simpler and more profound .... For many years, I simply told people not to waste their time reading all the other managerial leadership books. 'If you are really serious about the deeper territory of true leadership,' I would say, 'read Greenleaf.'[46]

While scholarly research is still at an early stage, the results so far indicate that servant leadership encourages positive organizational citizenship behaviors, creates a service climate at work, and promotes fairness in the workplace. Employees of servant-leaders are more helping and creative than those working with leaders who score lower on servant leadership. Servant leadership has been shown to be positively related to employee job satisfaction. Servant leadership also has a positive impact on employee commitment to the organization, job performance, and community citizenship behavior. Servant-leaders are good at building and facilitating effective teams. They promote open and problem-driven communication, team confidence, personal integrity, and cooperation among team members.[47]

In addition to expert opinion and scholarly research, we know that there are many companies using servant leadership principles that are doing very well indeed. For example, in 1998, *Fortune* magazine began publishing its list of "The 100 Best Companies to Work for in America." To qualify for the list today, companies must be at least seven years old and have at least 1,000 U.S. employees. Two-thirds of a company's score is based on a 57-question survey which is sent to a minimum of 400 company employees selected on a random basis. The survey asks about attitudes toward management, company philosophy and policies, job satisfaction, and camaraderie in the workplace.

The companies on the *Fortune* list are not only great places to work, they are also high-performance companies that deliver outstanding service and have strong financial returns. The shares of these companies out-perform the stock market, they have low turnover by industry standards, they continue to grow and create new jobs, and they have a bigger talent pool to draw from, because people want to work for them.

Over the years, a number of the top companies on the *Fortune* list have been implementing the principles of servant leadership. Those companies include TDIndustries, Southwest Airlines, Starbucks, Synovus Financial Corporation, Men's Wearhouse, Herman Miller, The Container Store, and AFLAC.

TDIndustries is an air conditioning, construction, and service company based in Dallas. TDIndustries has been implementing servant leadership principals for forty years. The company has been on the 100 Best Companies list for so many years that *Fortune* put the company into its 100 Best Companies "Hall of Fame." Jack Lowe, Jr., who led the company as CEO for twenty-four years, said:

In the past, we believed that being a great place to work would limit our ability to pay top wages, grow our business, and have outstanding financial performance. Our paradigm has shifted. We now believe that being a great place to work *allows* us to pay top wages, grow our business, and have outstanding career opportunities.[48]

Companies that take servant leadership seriously are great places to work, and that is a key element in their success. The ability to attract and keep good people is a strategic business advantage.

Key Practices

The real-world experience of organizations and the testimony of those who have spent decades studying leadership and management tell us that servant leadership really works. But why? Here are some key practices that help explain its effectiveness: self-awareness, listening, changing the pyramid, developing colleagues, coaching instead of controlling, unleashing the energy and intelligence of others, and the use of foresight.

1. Self-Awareness

We need to know what impact we are having on others, so that we can lead them well. As Kouzes and Posner point out in *A Leader's Legacy*, "What's crucial is that you become more self-aware—and self-awareness is a predictor of success in leadership."[49]

Servant-leaders are aware of their strengths and weaknesses. They know that they are not perfect, and yet they can perform at a high level; they know they have their own emotions and biases, and yet they can make wise and fair decisions. By building on their strengths and understanding their weaknesses, they are ready to build on the strengths and understand the weaknesses of others. They are less likely to judge, and more likely to encourage. They appreciate the importance of teams, in which each person is encouraged to contribute his or her strengths to the task at hand. They realize that every person and every job counts, and they treat every employee as a partner and colleague.

Self-awareness includes knowledge of the impact that one's words and deeds have on others. Servant-leaders are aware that saying one thing and doing another can destroy trust. Conversely, being true to your word, even when it is awkward or difficult, can build trust.

One of the hardest things to learn as a leader is that a grimace, an offhand remark, or a joke in poor taste can have a lasting negative impact on others. Conversely, a smile, a thoughtful remark, and an encouraging word can have a lasting positive impact.

Daniel Goleman and his co-authors point out in *Primal Leadership* that people look to the leader for emotional cues. "Emotion" in this sense is about feelings, tone, or mood, as well as strong emotions like happiness or anger. Leaders offer ways to interpret a given situation, and that includes their emotional reactions—the tone or mood of their response. Goleman reported on studies of working groups:

> ... [T]he impact on emotions goes beyond what a leader says. In these studies, even when leaders were not talking, they were watched more carefully than anyone else in the group. When people raised a question for the group as a whole, they would keep their eyes on the leader to see his or her response. Indeed, group members generally see the leader's emotional reaction as the most valid response, and so model their own on it—particularly in an ambiguous situation, where various members react differently. In a sense, the leader sets the emotional standard.[50]

Servant-leaders know that their moods are contagious. A servant-leader who projects a positive mood helps produce enthusiasm and cooperation among team members, which in turn produce success for the team.

Self-awareness arises from reflection. Isabel Lopez, who spent many years in business and then became a teacher of leaders, said:

> ... [O]nly through reflection do we find our purpose and the core of who we are. Reflection enables us to become our own teachers, and we never finish—never finish taking our own class, reading our own book, finding our own heart, and liberating our own spirit. Reflection forces us to face our own lives and beliefs .... Perhaps the greatest gift of reflection is that we ... can find the place that is true for us, the place where passion and serenity meet, both personally and professionally.[51]

Servant-leaders lead from self-awareness, and use the passion, serenity, and wisdom that come from reflection.

2. Listening

Servant-leaders identify and meet the needs of others. The first step toward identifying needs is to listen. Robert Greenleaf said that "only a true natural servant automatically responds to any problem by listening *first*."[52] He told the story of a very able leader who became the head of a large, complex public institution. When the leader realized after a short time that he was not happy with the way things were going, he focused on listening. Greenleaf reported:

> For three months he stopped reading newspapers and listening to news broadcasts; and for this period he relied wholly upon those he met in the course of his work to tell him what was going on. In three months his administrative problems were resolved. No miracles were wrought; but out of sustained intentness of listening that was produced by his unusual decision, this able man learned and received the insights needed to set the right course. And he strengthened his team by so doing.[53]

Servant-leaders gather feedback in as many ways as possible from their colleagues and those they serve. They listen to individuals face to face. They observe what people are doing. They ask questions. They conduct informal interviews, formal interviews, surveys, discussion groups, and focus groups. They use suggestion boxes. They do marketing studies and needs assessments. They are always asking, listening, watching, and thinking about what they learn. This is the foundation of their relevance and effectiveness.

The main point is this: Servant-leaders don't begin with the answer, the program, the product, the procedure, the facility. They don't begin with their own knowledge or expertise. They begin with questions that will help identify the needs of others. What do people say when asked about their needs, their wants, their hopes, their dreams? Servant-leaders watch and listen before they take action. They try hard to identify needs, before they try to meet them.

Taking time to identify needs is moral and respectful. It is also very practical. The simple fact is that *it is very hard to sell a product or service to people who don't want or need it.* If a servant-leader is good at identifying needs, he or she will be in a great position to meet those needs. If the servant-leader does in fact meet those needs, the servant-leader will be effective because he or she will be providing relevant products, programs, and services. That means that the servant-leader's organization will have many satisfied customers, clients, patients, members, or students. The organization will thrive, because the servant-leader listened, and made sure that what the organization offers is what people really *need*.

A problem faced by many organizations is that they are run by people who know a lot. Because they know a lot, they may not have the desire to learn *more*. But if they don't learn more, they simply won't know enough.

One of my favorite examples of this is Muhammad Yunus, who has changed the lives of hundreds of thousands of people in Bangladesh through micro-credit. In his book, *Creating a World without Poverty*, he describes how he was an economics professor, teaching about the nation's long-term plans. He was highly trained—he knew a lot about economic development. But things were not getting better. Finally, he went out into the villages of Bangladesh, and worked with the people, and listened, and discovered what he could do to change the relentless poverty of the country.

What he discovered was that people needed small amounts of capital. They had no collateral, so banks would not loan money to them. But the villagers were willing to work, and the amounts of capital they needed were very small. Yunus started by loaning his own money to people. His first forty-two loans came to a total of U.S. $27. People needed 50 cents or 70 cents to change their lives. Yunus asked for no collateral, but the villagers paid their loans back. He eventually established a bank, and started the mico-credit revolution.

Yunus has continued to watch and listen, and has launched an array of companies, each designed to give opportunities to the poor. It is an amazing story, which began with listening. By the way, the repayment rate over the last 20 years has been 98% to 99%, without collateral. It would have never happened if Yunus had not decided to listen first. He and his bank, Grameen Bank, won the 2006 Nobel Peace Prize for their work, which has spread to other parts of the world. [54]

Servant-leaders know that they have to keep listening, because people and situations change, and soon they can be "mostly right" but not right enough to develop the product or service that people really need. Servant-leaders ask themselves: How much do I really know about the needs of my colleagues and customers? How do I ask, and how often do I ask? Am I really listening? Am I open to hearing things I haven't heard before, as well as things I don't want to hear?

Richard Pieper is the Chairman of PPC Partners, Inc., headquartered in Milwaukee. PPC Partners owns a series of electrical service and construction firms. Dick joined Pieper Electric as President in 1960, when the family-owned business had eight employees doing $250,000 of business per year. Today, PPC Partners, Inc. employs 900 to 1,100 people, has sales in the hundreds of millions, and is one of the top electrical contracting firms in the United States.

One reason for the company's dramatic growth is that company leaders are good at getting feedback from colleagues and customers. They are always asking and listening. After every company semi-annual briefing, those who attended are asked to fill out an evaluation form that asks about the attendees' overall reaction to the meeting, pre-meeting communications, transportation, hotel, meeting room, food service (each meal), the program, and the chairman. They are asked what they enjoyed the most, and the least; what they learned and intend to implement; and what they recommend for future meetings. For regular meetings, there is a two-page "Post Meeting Reaction" form that asks similar questions. Dick even has a Chairman's Office Survey in which he asks each employee to rate him and his executive assistant on their quality of service, reliability, knowledge, and timeliness. Then, of course, there are regular surveys of customers. The comments are studied, and follow-up is comprehensive. At PPC Partners, listening is a high priority. It is a broad-based, systematic process with a focus on constant follow-up and improvement.

Part of the listening process consists of testing products or services in their early stages of development, to make sure they are aligned with customer needs. Years ago, when developing a new four-wheel, all-terrain vehicle (ATV), Suzuki Motor Company engineers took prototypes of the ATV to the apple orchards of Washington and asked the workers to try them out. The engineers watched and listened to the feedback they got from these early users. For example, the workers said they needed a basket for tools and insecticides, so the engineers added a basket.

Then they took the prototype to a local Suzuki dealer. He rode off, and was away a long time. The engineers began to worry. Did he have an accident? Did the prototype break down? Finally the manager returned with a big smile on his face. "That was fun!" he said. "I want to order twenty of these." It was only after listening and testing that the engineers knew that their product was ready to market.

3. Changing the Pyramid

The traditional organizational hierarchy is a pyramid. There are a few people at the top—the people who have power. Then there are more people in the middle, often known as middle managers. Most of the people are at the base of the pyramid. These are the people who create and deliver the products, programs, and services that the organization provides.

After 38 years of work at AT&T, Greenleaf concluded that the pyramidal structure doesn't work. In his essay, *The Institution as Servant,* he wrote:

> To be a lone chief atop a pyramid is *abnormal and corrupting.* None of us are perfect by ourselves, and all of us need the help and correcting influence of close colleagues. When someone is moved atop a pyramid, that person no longer has colleagues, only subordinates. Even the frankest and bravest of subordinates do not talk with their boss in the same way that they talk with colleagues who are equals, and normal communication patterns become warped .... The pyramidal structure weakens informal links, dries up channels of honest reaction and feedback, and creates limiting chief-subordinate relationships which, at the top, can seriously penalize the whole organization.

> A self-protective *image of omniscience* often evolves from these

warped and filtered communications. This in time defeats any leader by causing a distortion of judgment, for one's judgment is often best sharpened through interaction with others who are free to challenge and criticize.

Those persons who are atop the pyramids often suffer from a very real *loneliness*. They cannot be sure enough of the motives of those with whom they must deal, and they are not on the grapevine. Most of what they know is what other people choose to tell them. They often do not know what everybody else knows, informally.[55]

One solution is to broaden the top of the pyramid. Greenleaf recommended that organizations be led by teams in which the leader is not the boss but *primus inter pares*, or "first among equals."

Primus inter pares was the leadership model for universities founded in medieval Europe, at which faculty members gathered and elected one of their own as leader. The leader was expected to preside and guide as the equal of those who elected him. This ideal of collegial leadership is cherished by many faculty today.

I truly enjoyed being *primus inter pares* while chairing three accreditation teams in higher education. The teams consisted of accomplished professionals from different academic institutions who had university experience in a variety of areas such as academic programs, finance, information technology, student services, and governance. We would gather on the campus we were sent to evaluate, share our questions or concerns, and make plans. During the next two days, we would divide up and conduct individual meetings with faculty, students, staff, and administrators; research specific questions; and then reconvene to share what we had learned. Each member of the team would draft his or her own observations and conclusions, which I would compile into a single report. It was a "self-regulating" group that did not need a "boss." My role was to be the convener, the presider, the facilitator, and at the end of our visit, the spokesperson for the team.

One of the problems with the traditional pyramidal structure is that workers focus on pleasing their "bosses." Unfortunately, you can please your boss, and she can please hers, and he can please the board of directors, while nobody is really focused on *pleasing the customer*. When the pyramid is inverted, or tipped on its side, everyone in the organization can focus on pleasing customers, clients, members, or participants—the people whom the organization is designed to serve, and the people who will ultimately decide if the organization succeeds.

Bill Turner, who led the teams that built a number of companies, including Synovus Financial Corporation, said this:

> Based on the tenet that servant leadership is a commitment to love and serve, the organizational structure is turned upside down, with the leader at the bottom of the hierarchy, supporting those who do the work. The leader's primary responsibility is to meet the needs, whatever they may be, of those who serve the organization. It involves listening to others and together shaping a vision that everyone can own. The servant-leader becomes a funnel that creative ideas come to naturally from others who are themselves becoming servant-leaders. Servant-leaders are encouragers, communicators, and cheerleaders.[56]

Ken Blanchard, in his book *Leading at a Higher Level,* pointed out that servant-leaders stand at the top of the pyramid only when articulating the mission and vision of the organization, so everyone will know what direction the organization is going. After servant-leaders have listened and set the direction, their role changes. Blanchard said:

> Once people are clear on where they are going, the leader's role shifts to a service mindset for the task of implementation—the second aspect of leadership. How do you make the dream happen? *Implementation is where the servant aspect of servant leadership comes into play* .... Servant-leaders ... feel that their role is to help people achieve their goals. They constantly try to find out what their people need to perform well and live according to the vision.[57]

Steven B. Sample, former President of the University of Southern California, told a story in his book, *The Contrarian's Guide to Leadership*. At the tender age of thirty, he was named deputy director for academic affairs of the Illinois Board of Higher Education. The board's chairman, George Clements, was a successful business man.

Sample recalled that when he started work, Mr. Clements advised him to spend only 10 percent of his time hiring, evaluating, exhorting, praising, and motivating the people who reported directly to him. Clements said: "For the remaining 90 percent of your time you should be doing *everything you can* to help your direct reports succeed. You should be the first assistant to the people who work for you."[58] Clements told Sample to "work for those who work for you!" Sample has found this advice to be very valuable. He said:

> If you're not in the process of getting rid of a lieutenant, bend over backwards to help him get his job done. That means returning his phone calls promptly, listening carefully to his plans and problems, calling on others at his request, and helping him formulate his goals and develop strategies for achieving those goals. It's not simply that you should be your lieutenant's staff person, you should be his *best* staff person.[59]

In *The Servant Leader,* James Autry puts it this way: "One of the primary functions of the manager/leader is to assure that people get the resources they need to do the job. To be a leader who serves, you must think of yourself as—and indeed must be—their principal resource."[60]

4. Developing Your Colleagues

Greenleaf's best test of the servant-leader was: "Do those served grow as persons? Do they, *while being served*, become healthier, wiser, freer, more autonomous, more likely themselves to become servants?[61] Those served include one's colleagues. Helping them grow is a triple win: When your colleagues grow, the capacity of your organization grows, and the ability of your organization to serve others grows.

In his essay on "Servant Leadership in Business," Greenleaf proposed a new business ethic:

> Looking at the two major elements, the work and the person, the new ethic, simply but quite completely stated, will be: *the work exists for the person as much as the person exists for the work*. To put it another way, the business exists as much to provide meaningful work to the person as it exists to produce a product or service to the customer.

.... When the business manager who is fully committed to this ethic is asked, 'What are you in business for?" the answer may be: '*I am in the business of growing people* .... Incidentally, we also make and sell at a profit things that people want to buy so that we can pay for all this.'[62]

The TDIndustries "Mission Statement" is built on this ethic. The statement says: "We are committed to providing outstanding career opportunities by exceeding our customers' expectations through continuous aggressive improvement." The Mission Statement is elaborated by saying, "We believe in continuous, intense 'people-development' efforts, including substantial training budgets." The worker is as important as the work.

The Schneider Corporation in Indianapolis grew dramatically after it adopted servant leadership as a business philosophy twenty years ago. In its vision statement, the company sets forth its commitment to "challenging, encouraging and supporting one another so that we all grow personally and professionally." The company believes that servant leadership is a journey, and "servant-leaders are responsible for helping grow every person with whom they interact along their journey."

Since adults spend most of their waking hours at work, their workplaces have a huge impact on their personal growth and the meaning they find in life. Organizations have an ethical duty to provide workers with the opportunity to grow and find meaning. That is why servant-leaders offer learning experiences in the form of mentoring, training, new assignments, well-timed promotions, and broad-based experience in the organization. They keep track of the developmental needs and opportunities of their colleagues.

In *The Effective Executive*, Peter Drucker told the story of a company president whose contribution was the development of young managers at a large chain of retail stores. He was a "financial man" who had faithfully served in the number two slot in the company. When the CEO suddenly died, he became the new president. Even though he preferred working with numbers, he concluded that he could make the biggest difference by developing the company's managers. So three times a week he walked through the personnel department after lunch and picked up eight or ten file folders at random—the folders of young managers. Drucker reported:

> Back in his office, he opened the first man's folder, scanned it
> rapidly, and put through a telephone call to the man's superior. 'Mr.
> Robertson, this is the president in New York. You have on your staff
> a young man, Joe Jones. Didn't you recommend six months ago
> that he be put in a job where he could acquire some merchandising
> experience? You did. Why haven't you done anything about it?' And
> down would go the receiver.[63]

The president also called to congratulate supervisors for making sure that
their young managers got the experience they needed to continue growing.
Drucker said: "This man was in the president's chair only a few years
before he himself retired. But today, ten or fifteen years later, executives
who never met him attribute to him, and with considerable justice, the
tremendous growth and success of the company since his time." He simply
focused on developing people.[64]

The servant-leader takes great pleasure in helping others to grow and
become all that they can be. Stu Gothold was the Superintendent of the
Los Angeles County Schools, responsible for 4,000 employees and 1.6
million students in 82 districts. "I feel good when I help others succeed,"
Stu says. He likes a consensus style of decision-making. "I want to spend
time on a problem or topic, and give people the chance to get their
arms around it, so everyone has a piece of it," he says. "I want to make
sure I hear from the people who are working directly with the kids." He
acknowledges everybody as a member of the team. The reward of being
the team leader is seeing the achievements of all the team members.
"Years later, people still stay in touch," Stu says. "That has made it all
even more rewarding. I still hear from former students and colleagues."

Servant-leaders know that the mission of the organization is bigger
than any one person. By developing their colleagues, servant-leaders
improve not only the organization's performance today, but far into the
future. That is the servant-leader's legacy: A strong, vibrant team that is
trained and ready to take on any challenge, come what may.

5. Coaching, Not Controlling

In the power model, and many management textbooks, the assumption is that a leader or manager exercises power to "control" his or her unit or organization. The people who report to the manager constitute his or her "span of control." The manager's job is to "keep things under control."

James Showkeir is an organizational development expert who assists organizations in implementing servant leadership. He said: "The traditional belief is that, for the organization to succeed, organizational power should be entrusted to only a few at the top of the organization. The rest of the organization should comply with their directions and suffer the bureaucracy, even if it inhibits serving the customers."[65] A high price is paid for this kind of compliance. Showkeir pointed out:

> Compliance is not commitment. Compliance does not create passion. Compliance does not make individuals wiser. Compliance does not encourage choosing accountability. Compliance does not lead to creativity, flexibility, differentiation, and speed. Compliance does not create meaning and purpose. Compliance does not breed freedom. Meaning, purpose, and freedom ensue from struggle, risk, and engagement; compliance cuts us away from these.[66]

Servant-leaders are not focused on controlling their "subordinates." They do not measure their status in terms of their "span of control." They are not focused on compliance. Instead, they are focused on coaching and mentoring.

Kouzes and Posner note: "The more you control others, the more likely it is that they will rebel. Exemplary leaders have repeatedly told us that they get the greatest commitment precisely when they let their people go."[67] People do their best when they are taught, mentored, and coached, benefiting from both positive and negative feedback as they make their daily decisions and do their daily work.

In *The Servant Leader*, James Autry listed the six things he believes about leadership:

1. Leadership is not about controlling people; it's about caring for people and being a useful resource for people.

2. Leadership is not about being boss; it's about being present for people and building a community at work.

3. Leadership is not about holding on to territory; it's about letting go of ego, bringing your spirit to work, being your best and most authentic self.

4. Leadership is less concerned with pep talks and more concerned with creating a place in which people can do good work, can find meaning in their work, and can bring their spirits to work.

5. Leadership, like life, is largely a matter of paying attention.

6. Leadership requires love.[68]

Herb Kelleher, the former CEO of Southwest Airlines, said: "I have always believed that the best leader is the best server. And if you're a servant, by definition, you're not controlling."[69]

One reason that servant-leaders don't focus on controlling others is that *nobody really controls anybody else.* Each of us controls our own time and attention, but nobody else's. Yes, leaders can threaten, or persuade, or plead, but individuals have to decide if they are going to cooperate and respond to their leaders. Leaders may have "authority," but their followers have to accept and respond to that authority, or nothing will happen.

That was the message delivered by Chester Barnard back in the late 1930s. Barnard was a Bell Telephone executive, a man who knew something about business, education, government, and philanthropic organizations. In *The Functions of the Executive*, he argued that authority rests in the hands of the *receiver* of a communication. He said:

The necessity of the assent of the individual to establish authority for him is inescapable. A person can and will accept a communication as authoritative only when four conditions simultaneously obtain: *(a)* he can and does understand the communication; *(b) at the time of his decision* he believes that it is not inconsistent with the purpose of the organization; *(c) at the time of his decision*, he believes it to be compatible with his personal interest as a whole; and *(d)* he is able mentally and physically to comply with it.[70]

For the leader, then, giving orders is not enough. People need to understand, see the purpose, be in personal alignment, and be willing and able to do what is requested. You can't *make* them do that.

Servant-leaders know that people are not only capable of resisting an order—they are free to leave the organization and find a job somewhere else. Jack Lowe, Jr. of TDIndustries points out: "Your best employees have the talent and ability to leave your company and find work elsewhere if they want to. So you should lead them the way you lead volunteers."[71]

In addition to the difficulty of controlling people, a leader cannot control the organization's results through rigid organizational structures. One of the insights offered by Margaret Wheatley in *Leadership and the New Science* is that the universe can no longer best be understood as a machine, as in Newtonian physics. Rather, it is best understood in terms of relationships and connections, as in quantum physics. In mechanistic models, disruptions are seen as trouble. But in the new science, disorder can lead to new life and higher forms of order.

We should no longer expect our organizations to operate as machines we can control, but as dynamic living systems in which we can participate. We can lead by influencing and responding to the changes around us. We can support the emergence of new kinds of order that will work for us and our organizations. Servant-leaders thrive in an environment in which constant adjustment is necessary, because they are good at listening and identifying the changing needs.

The issue for the servant-leader is not how to control others, but how to build strong, positive relationships with others. Wheatley said:

> To live in a quantum world, to weave here and there with ease
> and grace, we will need to change what we do. We will need to
> stop describing tasks and instead facilitate process. We will need
> to become savvy about how to build relationships, how to nurture
> growing, evolving things. All of us will need better skills in listening,
> communicating, and facilitating groups, because these are the talents
> that build strong relationships .... Those who relate through coercion,
> or from a disregard for the other person, create negative energy.
> Those who are open to others and who see others in their fullness

create positive energy. Love in organizations, then, is the most potent source of power we have available.[72]

Servant leaders participate, guide, coach, and facilitate. They lead by identifying new sources of order and creating positive energy in their relationships.

6. Unleashing the Energy and Intelligence of Others

After developing and coaching their colleagues, servant-leaders encourage their colleagues to make more decisions on their own. Servant-leaders develop and coach their colleagues so that their colleagues will use their energy and intelligence wisely, for the good of the organization and those the organization serves.

Unleashing the energy and intelligence of others is a competitive advantage. As Stephen Covey said:

> You've got to produce more for less, and with greater speed than you've ever done before. The only way you can do that in a sustained way is through the empowerment of people. And the only way you get empowerment is through high-trust cultures and through the empowerment philosophy that turns bosses into servants and coaches .... Leaders are learning that this kind of empowerment, which is what servant leadership represents, is one of *the* key principles that, based on practice, not talk, will be the deciding point between an organization's enduring success or its eventual extinction.[73]

The importance of empowering cuts across different types of organizations. For example, Dan Ebener has conducted research on the impact of servant leadership at high-performing Catholic parishes. He focused on three servant leadership behaviors—recognizing, serving, and empowering. "Recognizing" includes acknowledging, affirming, and calling forth the gifts and talents of parishioners. "Serving" includes putting the needs and interests of others first. "Empowering" means involving the followers in making decisions that affect their own roles and goals within the organization. Ebener found that each of these behaviors, especially empowering leadership behaviors, supported high performance.[74] Servant leadership worked well at the parishes he studied.

Jack Lowe, Sr. founded Texas Distributors (now TDIndustries) in Dallas in 1946. When Greenleaf published his essay, *The Servant as Leader*, in 1970, Jack Lowe got a copy—and then bought more and more copies, sharing them in his company and throughout the community. Greenleaf called to find out why Lowe was buying so many copies, and that began a friendship between the two men. Lowe held discussion groups with employees to talk about Greenleaf's essay and how they might apply it at Texas Distributors. Out of those discussions grew a list of leadership values, including:

- Leaders are first a servant of those they lead. They are a teacher, a source of information and knowledge and a standard setter, more than a giver of directions and a disciplinarian.

- Leaders see things through the eyes of their followers. They put themselves in others' shoes and help them make their dreams come true.

- Leaders assume that their followers are working with them. They consider others Partners in the work and see to it that they share in the rewards. They glorify the team spirit!

- Leaders are people builders. They help those around them to grow because the leader realizes that the more strong people an organization has, the stronger it will be.

- Leaders do not hold people down, they lift them up. They reach out their hand to help their followers scale the peaks.

- Leaders have faith in people. They believe in them. They have found that others rise to their high expectations.

- Leaders can be led. They are not interested in having their own way, but in finding the best way. They have an open mind.[75]

These leadership values are about unleashing the energy and intelligence of everyone in the company.

Sometimes, a Partner at TDIndustries is not aligned with the company's values, and has to be asked to leave. One of the leadership values of the company states:

- Leaders are faced with many hard decisions, including balancing fairness to an individual with fairness to the group. This sometimes requires a 'weeding out' of those in the group who, over a period of time, do not measure up to the group needs of dependability, productivity and safety.

The hard decision has to be made, so that all Partners will be able to work well together in meeting the needs of customers.

Not unleashing the energy and intelligence of others is extraordinarily sad and wasteful. Most people work in service industries and perform knowledge work that requires individual decisions and judgments. Knowledge and skill are needed at all levels, and everyone counts. It doesn't make any sense to have lots of people in an organization, but let only a few people—those at the top—use their full potential. The people at the top of the pyramid can't *know* everything or *do* everything. They are only human; they have limits. Without participation and input from colleagues throughout the organization, they will make mistakes. Customers will be lost. Opportunities to develop new products and services will be lost.

In most organizations today, people are the biggest asset. The organization is paying for *all* its people. Why not engage them fully in the work at hand? Full engagement makes the organization more competitive, because it deploys more of its resources. The organization will be better able to understand and respond to the needs of colleagues and customers. Encouraging the full engagement of every member of the organization is also respectful: It shows confidence in the knowledge and skill of others. It sends a positive, inspiring message to those who interact with customers and make thousands of decisions each day that affect the future of the organization.

As James Showkeir pointed out, "the major problem with the traditional system is that it consolidates organizational power in places that have the least marketplace and customer contact. *Those with the most contact are the least powerful.*"[76] The energy and intelligence of those with the most contact must be unleashed for the organization to achieve its greatest possible success.

Howard Behar was one of the senior leaders who helped build Starbucks from twenty-eight stores to thousands of stores worldwide. He says that organizations should empower people to bring their unique perspectives and skills to the job. Leaders should also remember that those closest to the job are likely to have the best understanding of how to get the job done. "After all," Behar asks, "who is better equipped to choose the broom than the guy who sweeps the floor?"[77]

One way to unleash energy and intelligence is to build upon the intrinsic motivation of colleagues. Research done by Dr. Kenneth Thomas on motivation at work suggests that a sense of choice is a key intrinsic motivator.[78] A servant-leader who gives colleagues choices regarding the way they accomplish their work can unleash their intrinsic motivation. This is important, because research shows that people who are intrinsically motivated are more productive, more committed, more innovative, and less likely to burn out. According to Kouzes and Posner in their book, *The Leadership Challenge*, "external motivation is more likely to create conditions of compliance or defiance; self-motivation produces far superior results."[79]

Ken Melrose provides a good example of how to unleash the energy and intelligence of others. Melrose helped unleash his colleagues at Game Time, a subsidiary of the Toro Company that manufactured playground equipment. In 1973, at the age of thirty-two, Melrose was hired to lead the company.

The previous CEO was the founder of the company, and he made all the decisions. So when Melrose became president, the staff came to him, asking him questions and expecting *him* to make all the decisions. He declined. Instead, he asked them questions. If the staff member wanted to know how much steel to purchase, Melrose would ask him how much they bought in the last period, and how many merry-go-rounds they built with that amount of steel, and how many merry-go-rounds the sales manager thought they could sell in the next period, and how many merry-go-rounds they already had in stock, and so forth. He didn't tell them to do it on their own, and he didn't give them his own answer. Instead, he coached them with the questions until they could see how to work out the answers for themselves. Melrose recalled:

Over the three years I worked at Game Time, much of my effort was spent helping people learn processes for problem solving and decision making related to their jobs .... Bit by bit, I came to understand that you lead best by serving the needs of your people. You don't do their jobs for them; you enable them to learn and progress on the job. You multiply strengths as you empower and trust.[80]

During those three years, people began to enjoy their jobs. They had more confidence, more trust in each other, and they experienced better team work. Their sales increased 50 percent, their profits more than doubled, and Game Time was yielding the best return on investment of all of Toro's divisions. Later, in the early eighties, when the parent company was about to collapse, the board asked Melrose to become the CEO of all of Toro. He applied servant leadership principles in rebuilding and growing the company during the next twenty-two years.

7. Foresight

Greenleaf said that the central ethic of leadership is foresight. He said that "prescience, or foresight, is a better than average guess about *what* is going to happen *when* in the future."[81] Greenleaf said that a good leader has a high level of intuitive insight about the way the past and the present connect to the future. The servant-leader is "in every moment of time, historian, contemporary analyst, and prophet—not three separate roles."[82] Greenleaf said:

> Foresight is the 'lead' that the leader has. Once leaders lose this lead and events start to force their hand, they are leaders in name only. They are not leading, but are reacting to immediate events, and they probably will not long be leaders. There are abundant current examples of loss of leadership which stem from a failure to foresee what reasonably could have been foreseen, and from failure to act on that knowledge while the leader had freedom to act.[83]

Greenleaf said that the failure of a leader to foresee events may be viewed as an *ethical* failure, because a failure of foresight can put an organization in a bad situation that might have been avoided. Organizations tend to behave unethically when they are backed into a corner, and feel that they have no choices left except bad ones. Allowing an organization to get into that situation is itself an ethical failure.

Daniel Kim, an organizational consultant who has worked with America's largest corporations, distinguished between forecasting and foresight. He said:

> It would seem ... that the enormous complexity of our modern organizations leaves us incapable of exercising foresight, thereby sentencing us to be ethical failures as leaders. This would be true if we equated foresight with making accurate forecasts about the future (which is impossible to do). Fortunately for us, foresight is about being able to perceive the *significance and nature of events* before they have occurred (which is achievable).[84]

Kim shared an example used by Arie de Geus of Royal Dutch Shell:

> If it rains in the foothills of the Himalayas, we cannot forecast exactly when the rivers will swell and flood the valleys, but we can predict with certainty that the flooding will occur. The better we know the structure of the terrain, the greater knowledge we have about the flooding to follow. An ethical responsibility of a leader is to know the underlying structures within her domain of responsibility and be able to make predictions that can guide her people to a better future.[85]

Today, many leaders serve as CEOs for no more than a few years before retiring or moving to another position. As a result, many leaders are tempted to go for short-term gains, while ignoring long-term issues. They assume that they will be gone before the long-term issues become important, so they exercise little foresight. Unfortunately, the people who are still working in the organization, and those they serve, will suffer the disadvantages of the CEO's failure of foresight when the long-term issues become the central issues—or crises—years later.

Even when CEOs stay for the long term, they can fail to use foresight, and their organizations can suffer dismal consequences. In his book *Good to Great,* Jim Collins compared the Great Atlantic and Pacific Tea Company, known as A&P, with the Kroger grocery chain. In the 1950s, A&P was the largest retailing organization in the world, while Kroger was only about half as large. Both companies were old, both had nearly all their assets invested in traditional grocery stores, and both knew that the world was changing. In fact, both experimented with a new kind of "superstore."

However, fifty years later, A&P had faded away, and Kroger had pulled far ahead. The difference was that Kroger had foresight, and acted on it. Kroger concluded from its superstore experiment that the traditional grocery store would become extinct in the future. Kroger therefore eliminated, changed, or replaced every store and rebuilt its entire system on the new superstore model. By 1999, after years of spectacular growth, it had become the number one grocery chain in the United States.[86]

According to Noel Tichy and Warren Bennis in their book, *Judgment: How Winning Leaders Make Great Calls*, good judgment calls about the future are essential, and they require foresight. For example, in deciding where to lead General Electric in the future, CEO Jeff Immelt analyzed social, economic, and environmental trends and then began deciding what products or services to produce. Tichy and Bennis report that Immelt built his strategy on the assumption that the economy may grow more slowly and be more volatile; that to attract and motivate good people, GE will need to be more humane; and that GE can generate organic growth by using its research and technology base to develop new markets. Some of those markets will be in developing countries that need infrastructure, while in more advanced economies the opportunities are most likely to be in health care, in energy saving and production, and in environmentally friendly products.[87] Foresight in these areas became the basis for GE's business decisions for the future.

Joseph Jaworski led the scenario planning process at Royal Dutch Shell in the early 1990s. Shell had 120,000 employees in more than one hundred countries. Jaworski assembled a team to build the scenarios, and met with the company's most senior managers. As the process moved forward, it became clear that the global scenarios for the next thirty years would have to address the relationship between rich and poor countries. Two scenarios were finally developed—a pessimistic scenario they called "Barricades," which described an increasingly divided world with increased anarchy, and a more optimistic one they called "New Frontiers," which featured political and economic freedom for people around the world.

Jaworski observed that developing and sharing the scenarios changed the perceptions of those involved. In fact, rather than using the scenarios to react to events in the world when they occur, understanding the scenarios influenced how some people behaved *in advance of those events.* Jaworski concluded: "If individuals and organizations operate from the generative orientation, from possibility rather than resignation, we can *create* the future into which we are living, as opposed to merely reacting to it when we get there."[88] Exercising foresight can do more than prepare us for the future—it can help us create the future that we desire the most.

I had the honor and pleasure of serving in the cabinet of Hawaii Governor George Ariyoshi, a true public servant. Governor Ariyoshi was not only concerned about serving his community today—he worked hard to take into account future generations. He spent much of his time as a public servant trying to make life better for those who will come after us. His efforts were not focused on getting votes, because those who would most appreciate his efforts were not even born yet. His efforts were focused instead on creating our "preferred future." The interesting thing is that he was in political life for thirty years and never lost an election. People trusted him. People who met him and came to know him understood that he wasn't in it for himself, he was in it for the long-term good of the community.

Leaders with foresight can provide and maintain momentum in their organizations. This is something that leaders owe their colleagues and those they serve. In *Leadership Is an Art,* Max De Pree said:

> Leadership comes with a lot of debts to the future .... Momentum is one. Momentum in a vital company is palpable. It is not abstract or mysterious. It is the feeling among a group of people that their lives and work are intertwined and moving toward a recognizable and legitimate goal .... Momentum comes from a clear vision of what the corporation ought to be, from a well-thought-out strategy to achieve that vision, and from carefully conceived and communicated directions and plans which enable everyone to participate and be publicly accountable in achieving those plans.[89]

Leaders hold the future of their colleagues and customers in their hands. Foresight is needed to form the vision, create the plans, and generate the momentum that will make that future a good one for everyone.

5.

The Meaningful Lives
of Servant-Leaders

Why do people become servant-leaders? It may be that they have a natural desire to serve, or it may be that they hear the call as a result of their life experience. They spend years focused on their personal ambitions for power, wealth, and fame, and discover that such things are empty and meaningless compared with simple acts of service. It may be a result of their faith—they seek to follow the teachings of their religion. It may be that they love people, and simply want to help them. Whatever the case may be, they are committed to serving others.

That commitment is important, because servant-leaders are not always successful. Things may not go the way they had hoped, or people may not appreciate what they have done, or people may even criticize them for the good they are trying to do. But servant-leaders continue to help, no matter how difficult it may be.

Servant-leaders do not work to earn the appreciation of others. Appreciation may come their way, but it is not what motivates them. They derive a sense of meaning and satisfaction from doing a great job. It doesn't matter whether anybody else knows or appreciates what they do— *they* know. And that's enough.

Each of us likes to be appreciated. That's normal. But it is hard to be a servant-leader if you crave applause. Focusing on applause means that you are focused on yourself, not others. Servant-leaders focus instead on the meaning and satisfaction that they receive when they help others. That is something that nobody can take away from them. The meaning and satisfaction are theirs, whether anybody else applauds or not.

I was fortunate to learn this early in life. One of the real "aha!" experiences of my life occurred as I walked to the stadium for the student awards ceremony at my high school. It occurred to me that I was so happy about what I had done that year, and felt so good about what I had learned, and whom I had helped, that I didn't need any awards. *I had already been rewarded.* I already had the sense of meaning and satisfaction that came from doing a good job. That realization was a major breakthrough for me. I felt liberated. I felt an immense inner peace.

A couple of years later I was in college. It was the 1960s, a time of conflict and confrontation on many American college campuses. It was also a time of hope and high ideals. What disturbed me the most was watching idealistic young people go out into the world to do what they thought was right and good and true, only to come back a short time later, discouraged, or even embittered, because they didn't achieve the change they sought to achieve, or nobody seemed to appreciate what they were trying to do.

I was working with student leaders back then, and I had two basic messages for them. First, I told them that you really have to love people. You have to really care, because change usually takes time, and love is one of the only motivations that is strong enough to keep you with the people and with the process until change is achieved. The second message was this: If you go out into the world and do what you believe is right and good and true, then you will get a lot of meaning and satisfaction. If people appreciate you, that's fine, but if they don't, that's okay. *If you have the meaning, you don't have to have the glory.*

The Paradoxical Commandments

In my sophomore year in college, when I was 19, I wrote a booklet for high school student leaders. In that booklet I urged them to learn how to work with others to get things done. I challenged them with what I called "The Paradoxical Commandments of Leadership." This is what I wrote:

1. People are illogical, unreasonable, and self-centered.
   Love them anyway.

2. If you do good, people will accuse you of selfish ulterior motives.
   Do good anyway.

3. If you are successful, you will win false friends and true enemies. Succeed anyway.

4. The good you do today will be forgotten tomorrow. Do good anyway.

5. Honesty and frankness make you vulnerable. Be honest and frank anyway.

6. The biggest men and women with the biggest ideas can be shot down by the smallest men and women with the smallest minds. Think big anyway.

7. People favor underdogs but follow only top dogs. Fight for a few underdogs anyway.

8. What you spend years building may be destroyed overnight. Build anyway.

9. People really need help but may attack you if you do help them. Help people anyway.

10. Give the world the best you have and you'll get kicked in the teeth. Give the world the best you have anyway.[90]

The Paradoxical Commandments are guidelines for finding personal meaning in the face of adversity. That's why the first phrase in each commandment is about adversity, or difficulty, or disappointment: People are illogical, unreasonable, and self-centered. The good you do today will be forgotten tomorrow. People really need help, but may attack you if you do help them.

But each statement about adversity is followed by a positive commandment: Love people anyway. Do good anyway. Help people anyway.

The paradox is this. Even when the world is difficult—even when the world is *crazy*—you and I can still find personal meaning and deep happiness. We do that by facing the worst in the world with the best in ourselves.

The fact is that you and I, as individuals, can't control the external world. We can't control the world economy, and the rate of population growth. We can't control the weather, or natural disasters like fires and floods. We can't control when terrorists may strike or wars may break out. We can't control which companies will acquire which companies, and which jobs will be downsized and which jobs will open up. We can work hard, and prepare, and seize opportunities—and we should. We can join with others to influence those external events—and we should do that, too. But there are lots of things in our external world we just can't control.

What we can control is our inner lives. You and I get to decide who we are going to be and how we are going to live. We can live our most cherished values, and be close to our families and friends, and do what we know is right and good and true—no matter what. *No matter what.* The good news is that these are the things that have been giving people a lot of personal meaning for thousands of years.

Servant-leaders understand the Paradoxical Commandments. The Paradoxical Commandments focus on personal meaning, and so do servant-leaders. That is what makes it possible for them to keep working, whether they get applause, indifference, or even a negative response. They like to be treated well, but they are not especially concerned when they are treated badly. Servant-leaders are not worried about the attention others pay to them, but the attention they pay to others. That's where the meaning is to be found.

Meaning Is an Intrinsic Motivator

Finding meaning is important, because personal meaning is an intrinsic motivator. People are intrinsically motivated when they do something because they want to, not because they have to. They are intrinsically motivated when their work is interesting, and fulfilling, and meaningful. Research and common sense tell us that people who are intrinsically motivated are more productive, more innovative, more committed, and less likely to burn out than those who are extrinsically motivated. Since servant-leaders are intrinsically motivated, they have a big advantage over power-oriented leaders, who are extrinsically motivated.

Extrinsic motivation applies when people are motivated by something other than the work or activity itself. For example, a person who does her job not because she likes it, but as a way to get power or money, is extrinsically motivated.

Extrinsic rewards will always be important. We need to provide for ourselves and our families, so we care about salaries, benefits, bonuses, and awards. That's normal. But we want more than that, and need more than that, if we are to be productive, innovative, committed, and energized. We need to be intrinsically motivated.

Dr. Kenneth Thomas, who has done a great deal of research on motivation at work, points out:

> ... [S]tudies show that the intrinsic rewards are consistently related to job satisfaction and to performance. These findings hold across types of organizations and for managers as well as workers. Studies have also shown that the intrinsic rewards are related to innovativeness, commitment to the organization, and reduced stress.[91]

A sense of meaningfulness is an important intrinsic motivator at work. It is also very fundamental to our nature as human beings. Thomas said:

> There is a great deal of evidence that people are hardwired to care about purposes. We seem to need to see ourselves as going somewhere—as being on a journey in pursuit of a significant purpose .... There is also much evidence that people suffer when they lack purpose. Clinical studies show that people deteriorate in various ways without purpose.[92]

Dramatic testimony on this point came from Viktor Frankl in his book, *Man's Search for Meaning*. Frankl was a Jewish psychiatrist who survived the Nazi concentration camps in World War II. His story of life as a prisoner is a painful story of suffering and death. Prisoners had to work hard each day, with little food, clothing, sleep, or medicine in an environment of constant brutality and fear. Frankl observed that prisoners who had faith in the future, who still had a reason to live, were the ones who were most likely to survive. From this experience, he developed his theory of logotherapy, or meaning therapy, in which a patient is confronted with and reoriented toward the meaning of his life. Frankl believed that "striving to find a meaning in one's life is the primary motivational force in man."[93] That meaning varies from person to person, because each person's circumstances and tasks are different.

Bill Turner led the team that built Synovus Financial into the #1 Best Place to Work in America on the *Fortune* magazine list for 1999. In his book, *The Learning of Love: A Journey Toward Servant Leadership*, Turner mentioned many times his own search for meaning. Listening to Viktor Frankl lecture and reading his book, *Man's Search for Meaning*, were on Turner's list of experiences that shaped his life. Turner filled the emptiness in his soul with his faith, his love and compassion, and the meaning he derived from serving others.

Meaning Is Good for Mental Health

In addition to being more productive, more committed, more innovative, and less likely to burn out, people who are intrinsically motivated are also psychologically healthier.

Edward L. Deci wrote a book titled, *Why We Do What We Do: Understanding Self Motivation*. The book included a report on a study done on six types of life aspirations. Three were extrinsic—the aspiration to be wealthy, famous, and physically attractive. The other three were intrinsic—the aspiration to have meaningful personal relationships, to make contributions to the community, and to grow as individuals. Deci said:

> ... [S]trong aspirations for any of the intrinsic goals ... were positively associated with well-being. People who strongly desired to contribute to their community, for example, had more vitality and higher self-esteem. When people organize their behavior in terms of intrinsic strivings (relative to extrinsic strivings) they seem more content—they feel better about who they are and display more evidence of psychological health.[94]

The extrinsic goals were about what one *has*. The intrinsic goals were about who one *is*. The research showed that people who were heavily focused on extrinsic rewards had poor mental health.

This makes sense. If your goals are extrinsic, reaching them depends on the decisions of others and whims of fate over which you have no control. By contrast, reaching your intrinsic goals depends on your attitude, your values, and your work. Servant-leaders are focused on the intrinsic goal of identifying and meeting the needs of others. As a result, they have better mental health than many other kinds of leaders.

Meaning Is a Key to Deep Happiness

There is no question that finding personal meaning in life is also a key to being deeply happy. What do I mean by "deep happiness"? I mean the kind of happiness that touches your spirit and connects with your soul. It is hard to describe. Some people call it joy, or self-fulfillment, or self-actualization, or being centered. Others call it living their passion, or following their bliss. For people of faith, it may be finding the divine will for their lives, and then living that will. But however we describe it, personal meaning is a key.

In his book *Happiness: Lessons from a New Science*, Richard Layard stated that "people who achieve a sense of meaning in their lives are happier than those who live from one pleasure to another."[95] Layard quoted a study that showed that other factors that correlate with happiness and life satisfaction are autonomy, positive relationships, personal growth and self-acceptance.

Dennis Prager, in his book *Happiness Is a Serious Problem*, said that "happiness can be attained under virtually any circumstances providing you believe that your life has meaning and purpose."[96] Dan Baker and Cameron Stauth, in their book *What Happy People Know*, said that "happy people know why they're here on earth. They're doing the things they were meant to do. If they died today, they would be satisfied with their lives."[97]

Tal Ben-Shahar taught a popular course at Harvard on positive psychology. In his book *Happier*, he wrote that happiness is "the overall experience of pleasure and meaning."[98] Meaning comes from having a sense of purpose. He said:

> A happy person enjoys positive emotions while perceiving her life as purposeful. The definition does not pertain to a single moment but to a generalized aggregate of one's experiences: a person can endure emotional pain at times and still be happy overall.
>
> .... To live a meaningful life, we must have a self-generated purpose that possesses personal significance rather than one that is dictated by society's standards and expectations. When we do experience this sense of purpose, we often feel as though we have found our calling. As George Bernard Shaw said, 'This is the true joy of life, the being used for a purpose recognized by yourself as a mighty one.'[99]

By focusing on meaning, servant-leaders are intrinsically motivated, are psychologically healthier, and can find deep happiness.

Important Sources of Personal Meaning

There are at least four universal sources of personal meaning. These are four sources that are so fundamental that they cut across countries, cultures, and centuries. They can be found in most of the world's great religions and the teachings of many spiritual leaders. The four things you can do to find meaning are: Love people, help people, live ethically, and don't be too attached to material things.

I think there is a causal link between these four principles. If you love people, you will want to help them, and if you are loving and helping people, you will want to treat them right—you will want to treat them ethically. And if you are busy loving and helping others and treating them right, you are probably more focused on people than on things, so you probably aren't too attached to material things.

If I had to narrow it down even further, I would pick two core sources of meaning: (1) focus on others, and (2) become part of something larger than yourself. Focusing on others includes loving people, helping people, and treating them right. Becoming part of something larger than yourself is about joining with others in a team, an organization, a movement, a cause, a religion that makes a difference bigger than any of us can make as individuals. These sources of meaning are available to servant-leaders, every day.

"Symbols of Success" Are Not Enough

In our culture, leaders are rarely measured by how well they love people, help people, live ethically, and are not too attached to material things. Instead, they are usually measured by "symbols of success" like power, wealth, and fame.

What servant-leaders know is that the search for success and the search for meaning are not the same thing. They may overlap, but they are not the same. The things that our commercial, secular society considers to be attributes of success may have little to do with personal meaning.

For example, power is a symbol of success. But people learn that there is more meaning in helping people than in ordering them around. Wealth is a big symbol of success. But even the wealthy discover that there is more meaning in appreciating the richness of daily life—family, friends, hobbies, sunsets. Fame is a symbol of success, but the famous know that there is more meaning in being intimately known to a few people than being superficially known to millions of people. Winning is a symbol of success, but people learn that there is more meaning in always doing their personal best, win or lose.

The symbols of success are not necessarily bad. They're just *not enough*. It is not enough to get ahead. We also need to get meaning. This point was made dramatically by Edwin Arlington Robinson in his poem "Richard Cory."

Whenever Richard Cory went down town,
    We people on the pavement looked at him:
He was a gentleman from sole to crown,
    Clean favored, and imperially slim.

And he was always quietly arrayed,
 And he was always human when he talked;
But still he fluttered pulses when he said,
 "Good morning," and he glittered when he walked.

And he was rich—yes, richer than a king,
 And admirably schooled in every grace:
In fine, we thought that he was everything
 To make us wish that we were in his place.

So on we worked, and waited for the light,
 And went without the meat, and cursed the bread;
And Richard Cory, one calm summer night,
 Went home and put a bullet through his head.

We need more meaning in our lives than the "symbols of success" can provide. That is what I finally came to understand about Albert Schweitzer. He has been one of my heroes since I was a boy. Albert Schweitzer was one of the most brilliant and accomplished Europeans of his day. Born in 1875 in Alsace, Schweitzer distinguished himself early as an outstanding musician, philosopher, and theologian. Then, at age thirty, he began to study medicine and surgery to prepare for what he called "the direct service of humanity." In 1913, when he was thirty-eight, he and his wife left their comfortable lives in Europe and sailed to Western Africa, where they set up a crude hospital.

In their first year, the Schweitzers and their aides served over two thousand patients suffering from such diseases as malaria, yellow fever, and leprosy. Over the years, Schweitzer traveled to Europe and America to lecture and raise money for the hospital. He continued to serve others and promote his concept of reverence for life until his death in 1965.

I am impressed that Schweitzer gave up "success" for service. But I now realize that he gained more than he gave up.

Some people say that servant leadership is about giving up one's self-interest. They think a life of servant leadership is about self-sacrifice or self-denial. I disagree. *Servant leadership is not about self-sacrifice or self-denial. It is about self-fulfillment.* It is about living closely to your most important sources of meaning, and thereby finding more meaning and deep happiness than are available in any other way.

Each of us has talents and abilities, and we should use them to the fullest. There is no point in going out into the world each day to fail. Servant-leaders work hard, and when they do, they are often "successful." But servant-leaders know that the symbols of success do not give them the deep happiness that comes from the most important sources of meaning in their lives and work.

Being Counter-Cultural

Of course, staying focused on the important sources of meaning in life can be "counter-cultural." TV and radio programs, movies, magazines and newspapers all promote the symbols of success. People who don't have these symbols of success are judged to be failures.

Robert Greenleaf knew that "to the worldly, servant-leaders may seem naïve .... [S]ervant-leaders may stand alone, largely without the support of their culture, as a saving remnant of those who care for both persons and institutions, and who are determined to make their caring count—*wherever they are involved.*"[100]

What our culture does not understand is that a "worldly" leader who seeks power, wealth, and fame, is not likely to be relevant or effective, and therefore, is not likely to be good for society. The "successful" leader will be focused on accumulating power, wealth, and fame, instead of identifying and meeting the needs of others. The symbols of success are a distraction that shifts the focus away from the needs of the organization and society at large. Thus, a "successful" leader may be a failure in terms of solving problems and seizing opportunities that will make the world a better place.

The most effective leaders do not seek power, wealth, or fame—they seek to make a difference in the lives of others. Paradoxically, when they *do* make a difference in the lives of others, they are often *given* power, wealth and fame. However, when that happens, they treat their power, wealth, and fame as tools to be used in helping others.

Personally Committed, Spiritually Liberated

One reason that people live a life of servant leadership is that it allows them to be personally committed and spiritually liberated. They make strong personal commitments to the mission and goals of their organizations. They bring their spirit and soul with them to fulfill those commitments. However, they are spiritually free. They love people and work hard to help them. But their organizations don't "own" them.

If servant-leaders were focused on the symbols of success that the organization can give or deny them, they might be at the mercy of the organization. But they are not focused on the symbols of success, so they are free from the coercive impact of those extrinsic motivators.

A servant-leader seeks opportunities to use his or her talents in service to others. Organizations are a great place to do that. Almost nothing in today's world is accomplished alone. We achieve more by working in teams.

However, a servant-leader is not afraid to leave an organization and seek a new way to serve, or even a new life, somewhere else. The paradox is that *this freedom to leave the organization gives dignity and meaning to the servant-leader's decision to stay.* When you know that you can leave and start a new life elsewhere, you go to work each day to freely give your time and talent. You aren't there because you are trapped and have to "do your time" until you retire. You are there to give the gifts you can give to help your organization succeed in serving others.

Work gives each employee a label, income, and status. It gives each employee a set of colleagues and the opportunity to make a difference in the world. But if your job is all that defines you, you may suffocate. You may do and say only those things that your boss or your organization wants you to do and say, because you can't imagine losing your job. Each day you go along, keep your head down, give in, and try to survive, even though something inside you is dying. You are fearful, clinging to the only job you know, afraid that you might lose it, and suffering a deep sadness because you do not have the courage to change your circumstances.

This is critically important. If your job is all that defines you, you will be tempted to "sell out" when a moral conflict arises, or you will be tempted to cling to your job even when your spiritual life is dying. Obviously, you will not be your best—you will not lead others with enthusiasm and confidence—if you are selling out or your spirit is dying.

In secular terms, spirit can be defined as "an attitude or principle that inspires, animates, or pervades thought, feeling, or action." You need to do things that inspire and animate you. You also need to bring your soul to work. In everyday language, soul can be defined as "the spiritual part of humans regarded in its moral aspect." You can't afford to lose your soul.

How do you achieve the freedom to leave for another position or start a new life? You achieve it by being bigger than your job—by defining yourself more broadly than the work you do for your organization. You define yourself in terms of your family, your friends, your faith, your values, your skills, your hobbies, your passions, your dreams. Your work gives you the opportunity to give of yourself, but your work is not your self. You are more than your job.

Knowing that you can find another leadership position, or even a new life elsewhere, gives you the freedom to be honest and authentic with others. You can speak the truth, and do what needs to be done, even when it puts your job at risk. You know that the worst thing is not losing your job. The worst thing is losing your spirit and your soul.

In his book *The Heart Aroused*, David Whyte tells the story of a friend who was in a meeting in which the CEO of his company asked the senior executives for their opinion of a plan that the CEO wanted to implement. He asked them to rate his plan on a scale of one to ten. It was clear that he was tired of people resisting his ideas. He wanted everyone in the room to give the plan a ten.

Whyte's friend knew that the plan was terrible, and everyone in the company would lose by it. He also knew that half the executives in the room understood that it was a bad plan. But as the CEO went around the room, calling on each executive, most of them gave the plan a ten. One gave it a nine and a half. Whyte's friend was the last to speak. Whyte says: "He reaches his hand toward the flame, opens his palm against the heat, and suddenly falters; against everything he believes, he hears a mouselike, faraway voice, his own, saying *'ten.'*"[101]

If he had said *zero*, he would have risked dismissal, or perhaps a slow lingering "death" on the sidelines of his organization. Whyte says that his friend said "ten" because he was not ready for a life somewhere else. He was afraid. And so he did something that diminished his spirit.

Perhaps he could have been more clever. Perhaps he could have given the CEO constructive suggestions about how to improve the plan to make it a "ten." But it might not have made a difference. The CEO wanted obedience, not honesty. He wanted "tens," not new ideas. Whyte's friend still might have ended up looking for another job, or languishing in the one he had.

These situations are never easy. But servant-leaders know they cannot do and be their best when their spirit and soul are being strangled. They are committed to service, so when the situation does not allow them to fulfill that commitment, they seek to serve elsewhere.

To thrive as a servant-leader, you don't need symbols of success. You need to get material results for your organization, but you need spiritual returns for yourself. You need the personal meaning that will feed your spirit and your soul and give you deep happiness. You need the kind of happiness that cannot come from power, wealth, or fame. You need the happiness that can only come from a life of service.

Postscript

And so I return to the point at which I began: There does not have to be so much pain and suffering, so much war and violence, so much starvation and disease, so many crushed dreams and untapped talents, so many problems unsolved and so many opportunities ignored. *The world does not have to be like this.*

Greenleaf said: "Servant-leaders differ from other persons of goodwill because they act on what they believe. Consequently, they 'know experimentally' and there is a sustaining spirit when they venture and risk."[102] With that sustaining spirit, servant-leaders can change the world. Many have already changed it; more are changing it today.

Changing the world for the better has never been easy. It not only takes hard work, it takes a dream. Greenleaf said:

> For anything to happen there must be a dream. And for anything great to happen there must be a great dream .... One of these great dreams is for the good society made up of predominantly serving institutions that shape its character by encouraging serving individuals and providing scope and shelter for large creative acts of service—by individuals and groups.[103]

Our dreams can reshape our world. Not all dreams come true; and if our dreams are big enough, they will not come true in our lifetimes. But we can still find meaning and deep happiness working toward our dreams.

Over the past thirty years, I have come to understand that *service is not just something you do. It's what life is about.* Nothing is more important, or more meaningful and fulfilling, than loving and helping others.

Albert Schweitzer said: "I don't know what your destiny will be, but one thing I know: the only ones among you who will be really happy are those who will have sought and found how to serve."

I wish you that happiness!

Questions for Reflection and Discussion

Chapter 1: It Starts With the Desire to Serve

1. Do you agree that service is considered to be important by the world's great religions and thinkers? If so, why do you think this is true? If not, why not?

2. Robert Coles said that "all service is directly or indirectly ethical activity, a reply to a moral call within, one that answers a moral need in the world." Do you agree? If so, why? If not, why not?

3. How do you serve others in your family, your school, your organization, or your community?

4. How does service to others give you "satisfactions"?

5. What is your opinion of people who devote a significant part of their lives to serving others?

6. What are three specific ways you can expand your service to others? Start one this week.

7. How can you remain focused on the needs of others?

Chapter 2: Who is a Servant-Leader?

1. How would you define a servant-leader? Write your own definition.

2. Name servant-leaders you know from history, literature, or real life today. What is it that makes them servant-leaders?

3. Name some famous leaders who were not servant-leaders. Why weren't they?

4. Read *Profiles in Courage* by John F. Kennedy. Which of the Senators in the book were servant-leaders? Explain.

5. In defining the servant-leader, Greenleaf said that the best test is: "Do those served grow as persons? Do they, *while being served,* become healthier, wiser, freer, more autonomous, more likely themselves to become servants? And, what is the effect on the least privileged in society? Will they benefit or at least not be further deprived?" Are there times when you have met this test? When and how?

Chapter 3: Power Model vs. Service Model

1. How would you define the power model of leadership?

2. How would you define the service model of leadership?

3. Make two columns and head one "power model" and the other one "service model." In each column, list words that describe each model. Which words are the same for both columns, and which are different?

4. To what end does a power-oriented leader use power? To what end does a servant-leader use power?

5. Which model of leadership have you used *most often?* Why?

6. Greenleaf said that serving each other requires love. He noted that love is undefinable. "But it begins, I believe, with one absolute condition: unlimited liability!" What does "unlimited liability" mean to you?

7. How does love become real in serving others?

8. Do you agree that serving others requires community?

Chapter 4: The Key Practices of Servant-Leaders

1. Do you think servant leadership works in all sectors—public, private, non-profit, and academic? Why or why not?

2. Are there ways in which any organization, in any sector, can contribute toward building a better society through servant leadership?

3. What are the specific practices of servant leadership?

4. Which practices make the most sense to you? Which make the least sense?

5. Which practices do you think are the hardest? The easiest?

6. Why is listening an important practice of servant-leaders?

7. How do you interpret the statement that servant-leaders don't begin with the answer?

8. What are the advantages of changing the traditional pyramidal hierarchy?

9. What does it mean to work for those who work for you?

10. Have you ever worked for a "boss" who was "controlling"? If so, how did you feel about your work?

11. Have you ever worked with a leader who was your "coach"? If so, how did you feel about your work?

12. Do you agree that foresight is the "lead" that the leader has?

Chapter 5: The Meaningful Lives of Servant-Leaders

1. Why do you think people become servant-leaders?

2. Why do you think people remain servant-leaders?

3. What is most attractive about servant leadership to you?

4. What is least attractive about servant leadership to you?

5. Do you believe in doing what is right and good and true, *anyway?* If so, why? If not, why not?

6. Are you more intrinsically motivated, or more extrinsically motivated? How do you know?

7. Do you think servant leadership is about self-denial and self-sacrifice, or about self-fulfillment? Why?

8. Have you experienced deep happiness in your life? When, and why?

9. Do you think that servant leadership is counter-cultural? Why, or why not?

10. What role does courage play in remaining a servant-leader? What kind of courage?

Appendix: Servant Leadership Compared with Other Ideas

Robert Greenleaf published his classic essay, *The Servant as Leader*, in 1970. He revised and republished it in 1973. Since then, there have been many new ideas or theories about leadership. How do these ideas or theories compare, or overlap, with servant leadership?

The answer depends partly on how you define servant leadership and how you define the other ideas or theories. In recent years, scholars have become interested in developing a theory of servant leadership in order to test it and compare it with other leadership theories. Based on the views of a number of scholars, the elements that are most unique to servant leadership compared with other theories are:

(1) the moral component, not only in terms of the personal morality and integrity of the servant-leader, but also in terms of the way in which a servant-leader encourages enhanced moral reasoning among his or her followers, who can therefore test the moral basis of the servant-leader's visions and organizational goals;

(2) the focus on serving followers for their own good, not just the good of the organization, and forming long-term relationships with followers, encouraging their growth and development so that over time they may reach their fullest potential;

(3) concern with the success of all stakeholders, broadly defined— employees, customers, business partners, communities, and society as a whole—including those who are the least privileged; and

(4) self-reflection, as a counter to the leader's hubris.[104]

A detailed comparison of servant leadership with other theories was published by Dirk van Dierendonck in the *Journal of Management*. He established six characteristics of servant-leaders, and then used them in his comparison (see Table 1). The six characteristics are: (1) empowering and developing people; (2) humility; (3) authenticity; (4) interpersonal acceptance; (5) providing direction; and (6) stewardship. Van Dierendonck compared these characteristics with the characteristics of seven leadership theories that he believed revealed the most overlap with servant leadership. Those theories were transformational leadership, authentic leadership, ethical leadership, Level 5 leadership, empowering leadership, spiritual leadership, and self-sacrificing leadership.

In comparing servant leadership with transformational leadership, van Dierendonck pointed out that servant leadership focuses on humility, authenticity, and interpersonal acceptance, none of which are explicit in transformational leadership. More specifically, transformational leaders focus on organizational objectives, while servant leaders focus more on concern for their followers. Van Dierendonck believes that authentic leadership could be incorporated into servant leadership, because it overlaps with servant leadership on two characteristics, authenticity and humility. However, servant leaders work for all stakeholders, whereas authentic leaders might focus on a single stakeholder, like shareholders.

Three servant leadership characteristics overlap with ethical leadership—empowering and developing people, humility, and stewardship. However, the other three characteristics of servant leadership—authenticity, interpersonal acceptance, and providing direction—are relatively unimportant in ethical leadership. Servant leadership overlaps with Level 5 leadership in humility and providing direction. However, elements like authenticity, interpersonal acceptance, and stewardship are clearly missing from the definition of Level 5 leadership.

The first characteristic of servant leadership, empowering and developing people, obviously overlaps with empowering leadership. However, empowering leadership does not include any of the other five characteristics of servant leadership. Van Dierendonck notes that it is unclear what behavior follows from spiritual leadership, so it is not clear how servant leadership and spiritual leadership might overlap. As for self-sacrificing leadership, he said that it is rooted in transformational

Table 1

Dr. Dirk van Dierendonck's comparison of his six characteristics of servant leadership with the characteristics of other leadership theories

Leadership theories	*Six characteristics of servant leadership*					
	Empowering	Humility	Authenticity	Interpersonal Acceptance	Providing Direction	Stewardship
Servant leadership	yes	yes	yes	yes	yes	yes
Transformational	yes				yes	yes
Authentic		yes	yes			
Ethical	yes	yes				yes
Level 5		yes				
Empowering	yes				yes	
Spiritual*						
Self-sacrificing**	[yes]				[yes]	[yes]

*Behaviors of spiritual leadership are unknown, so it is not known how it would overlap

**Based on transformational leadership, and therefore presented in brackets

Van Dierendonck concluded that none of the seven theories incorporates all six characteristics of servant leadership, which puts servant leadership in a unique position. Additionally, servant leadership theory distinctly specifies a combined motivation to be(come) a leader with a need to serve that is at the foundation of these behaviors, and it is most explicit in emphasizing the importance of follower outcomes in terms of personal growth without necessarily being related to organizational outcomes.

From Dirk van Dierendonck, "Servant Leadership: A Review and Synthesis," *Journal of Management*, 2010. Table courtesy of Courtney Knies.

leadership, and different from servant leadership in its focus on the organization instead of the followers.

Van Dierendonck concluded that none of the seven theories incorporates all six of the characteristics of servant leadership, which puts servant leadership in a unique position. Additionally, servant leadership theory distinctly specifies a combined motivation to be(come) a leader with a need to serve that is at the foundation of these behaviors, and it is most explicit in emphasizing the importance of follower outcomes in terms of personal growth without necessarily being related to organizational outcomes.

Many people see the similarities between servant leadership and transforming leadership, as originally defined by James MacGregor Burns in his Pulitzer-Prize winning book, *Leadership*. Burns identified two basic types of leadership—transactional and transforming. He said:

> The relations of most leaders and followers are *transactional*— leaders approach followers with an eye to exchanging one thing for another: jobs for votes, or subsidies for campaign contributions. Such transactions comprise the bulk of the relationships among leaders and followers, especially in groups, legislatures, and parties. *Transforming* leadership, while more complex, is more potent. The transforming leader recognizes and exploits an existing need or demand of a potential follower. But, beyond that, the transforming leader looks for potential motives in followers, seeks to satisfy higher needs, and engages the full person of the follower. The result of transforming leadership is a relationship of mutual stimulation and elevation that converts followers into leaders and may convert leaders into moral agents.[105]

Burns suggested that the best modern example of a transforming leader was Gandhi, "who aroused and elevated the hopes and demands of millions of Indians and whose life and personality were enhanced in the process."[106]

Bernard Bass replaced the "transforming leader" described by Burns with the "transformational leader" mentioned above. A transformational leader inspires followers with a compelling mission and a vision, attends to their needs, and acts as a mentor or coach, drawing out their intrinsic motivation. A transformational leader encourages creativity and independent thinking, challenges the status quo, and serves as a role model of ethical behavior.

Jill W. Graham, in an article in *Leadership Quarterly*, and Mark Ehrhart, in an article in *Personnel Psychology*, compared servant leadership and transformational leadership. They argued that servant leadership defines stakeholders more broadly, even including the least privileged; encourages followers to enhance their moral reasoning capacities, so they can test the morality of the leader's visions and objectives; and serves followers for their own good as well as the good of the organization. As noted above, Van Dierendonck found that a transformational leader did not have the characteristics of humility, authenticity, and interpersonal acceptance that were included in his definition of servant leadership.

Many people see similarities between servant leadership and the Level 5 leaders described by Jim Collins in his book *Good to Great*. Level 5 is the highest level in his hierarchy of executive capabilities. Collins said:

> Level 5 leaders channel their ego needs away from themselves and into the larger goal of building a great company. It is not that Level 5 leaders have no ego or self-interest. Indeed, they are incredibly ambitious—but their ambition is first and foremost for the institution, not themselves.[107]

In his research, Collins found that the most effective leaders were both modest and willful, both humble and fearless. In interviews, the Level 5 leaders didn't talk about themselves, they talked about their companies and the contributions of other executives. Collins said that "the good-to-great leaders never wanted to become larger-than-life heroes. They never aspired to be put on a pedestal or become unreachable icons. They were seemingly ordinary people quietly producing extraordinary results."[108] While being modest, Level 5 leaders had "ferocious resolve, an almost stoic determination to do whatever needs to be done to make the company great."[109]

It is reported that some of the researchers working with Collins suggested using the name "servant-leader" instead of Level 5 leader. Van Dierendonck argues that servant leadership and Level 5 leadership share the elements of humility and providing direction, but servant leadership elements like authenticity, interpersonal acceptance, and stewardship are not part of the definition of Level 5 leadership.

Servant leadership has elements in common with the ideas of stewardship and co-leadership. Peter Block, in his book *Stewardship*, proposed replacing the concept of leadership with the concept of stewardship. He said that stewardship is "the willingness to be accountable for the well-being of the larger organization by operating in service, rather than in control, of those around us."[110] Authentic service exists when there is a balance of power, the primary commitment is to the larger community, each person joins in defining purpose and deciding what kind of culture the organization will become, and there is a balanced and equitable distribution of rewards.

Stewardship involves partnership rather than patriarchy, and empowerment instead of dependency. This requires the deepening of one's commitment to service instead of self-interest. Block wrote:

> The antidote to self-interest is to commit and to find a cause .... Let the commitment and cause be the place where we work. It is not so much the product or service of our workplace that will draw us out of ourselves. It is the culture and texture and ways of creating community that attract our attention. Our task is to create organizations we believe in and to do it as an offering, not a demand.[110]

In their book *Co-Leaders: The Power of Great Partnerships*, David Heenan and Warren Bennis described the essential roles played by people who are not the stars or celebrities in their organizations, but rather key subordinates—deputies, chief operating officers, or vice presidents who are committed, skilled, supportive partners and members of the leadership team. "We know that every successful organization has, at its heart, a cadre of co-leaders—key players who do the work, even if they receive little of the glory."[112] They observed that in co-leadership:

> Power and responsibility are dispersed, giving the enterprise a
> whole constellation of costars—co-leaders with shared values and
> aspirations, all of whom work together toward common goals
> .... Successful costars are consummate team players and, thus,
> valuable models for everyone interested in effective collaboration.
> Usually servant-leaders, they tend to be self-reliant, yet committed
> to organizational goals .... Outstanding co-leaders know that they
> don't have to be at the top of the organizational chart to find
> satisfaction— that exercising one's gifts and serving a worthy cause
> are far more reliable sources of satisfaction than the title on one's
> office door.[113]

It is important to remember that Greenleaf did not propose servant
leadership as an academic theory, but as a philosophy with a set of
practices. The importance of serving others is recognized throughout
the world. As Stephen Prosser noted in his essay, *Servant Leadership: More
Philosophy, Less Theory,* Greenleaf did not invent the concept of service.
However:

> ... [Greenleaf] articulated, as a new and appropriate voice within
> the twentieth century (and for the twenty-first century and beyond),
> a concept that has been the bedrock of civilized and compassionate
> existence for centuries. Greenleaf's major contribution has been to
> show that this principle, this philosophy of life in general, can exist
> and have credence within modern organizational life .... To treat
> servant leadership as if it were only another general leadership
> theory runs the risk of missing the full depth of Greenleaf's
> thinking, devaluing the philosophical, moral, spiritual, historical,
> cultural and intellectual fascination inherent in his work." (pp.40-
> 41)

Prosser concluded that if one needed to create a theory to explain
Greenleaf's writings, it would not be a theory of leadership, it would be a
theory of servanthood.

Sources

James A. Autry, *The Servant Leader: How to Build a Creative Team, Develop Great Morale, and Improve Bottom-Line Performance* (Roseville, California: Prima Publishing, 2001).

Dan Baker and Cameron Stauth, *What Happy People Know: How the New Science of Happiness Can Change Your Life for the Better* (Emmaus, Pennsylvania: Rodale, Inc., 2003).

Chester I. Barnard, *The Functions of the Executive* (Cambridge, Massachusetts: Harvard University Press, 1966).

Howard Behar, *It's Not About the Coffee: Leadership Principles from a Life at Starbucks* (New York: Penguin Group, 2007).

Tal Ben-Shahar, *Happier: Learn the Secrets to Daily Joy and Lasting Fulfillment* (New York: McGraw Hill, 2007).

Ken Blanchard, "Foreword: The Heart of Servant Leadership," in Larry C. Spears and Michele Lawrence, eds., *Focus on Leadership: Servant Leadership for the Twenty-First Century* (New York: John Wiley & Sons, Inc., 2002).

Ken Blanchard and the Founding Associates and Consulting Partners of the Ken Blanchard Companies, *Leading at a Higher Level: Blanchard on Leadership and Creating High Performing Organizations* (Upper Saddle River, New Jersey: Blanchard Management Corporation Publishing as Prentice Hall, 2007).

Ken Blanchard, Scott Blanchard, and Drea Zigarmi, Chapter 12, "Servant Leadership," in Ken Blanchard and the Founding Associates and Consulting Partners of the Ken Blanchard Companies, *Leading at a Higher Level: Blanchard on Leadership and Creating High Performing Organizations* (Upper Saddle River, New Jersey: Blanchard Management Corporation Publishing as Prentice Hall, 2007).

Peter Block, *Stewardship: Choosing Service Over Self-Interest* (San Francisco: Berrett-Koehler Publishers, 1993).

Juana Bordas, *Salsa, Soul, and Spirit: Leadership for a Multicultural Age* (San Francisco: Berrett-Koehler Publishers, Inc., 2007).

James MacGregor Burns, *Leadership* (New York: Harper & Row, Publishers, 1978).

Robert Coles, *The Call of Service* (Boston: Houghton Mifflin Company, 1993).

Jim Collins, *Good to Great: Why Some Companies Make the Leap ... and Others Don't* (New York: HarperCollinsPublishers, 2001).

Stephen Covey, "Foreword: Servant Leadership from the Inside Out," in Larry C. Spears, ed., *Insights on Leadership: Service, Stewardship, Spirit, and Servant Leadership* (New York: John Wiley & Sons, Inc., 1998).

Edward L. Deci, *Why We Do What We Do: Understanding Self-Motivation* (New York: G. P. Putnam's Sons, 1995).

Max De Pree, *Leadership Is an Art* (New York: Doubleday, 1989).

Peter F. Drucker, *The Effective Executive* (New York: Harper & Row, Publishers, 1967).

Eknath Easwaran, trans., *The Bhagavad Gita* (Tomales, California: Nilgiri Press, 1985).

Dan R. Ebener, *The Servant Parish: A Case Study of Servant Leadership and Organizational Citizenship Behaviors in High-Performing Catholic Parishes* (Dissertation presented to the Doctoral Faculty Council of St. Ambrose University in partial fulfillment of the requirements for the degree Doctor of Business Administration, May 2007.) See also, Dan Ebener, *Servant Leadership Models for Your Parish* (New York: Paulist Press, 2010).

Mark G. Ehrhart, "Leadership and Procedural Justice Climate as Antecedents of Unit-Level Organizational Citizenship Behavior, *Personnel Psychology*, 57, 61-94 (2004).

Joseph J. Ellis, *Founding Brothers: The Revolutionary Generation* (New York: Vintage Books, 2000).

Ezekiel, in *The Holy Bible*, New International Version (Grand Rapids, Michigan: Zondervan Bible Publishers, 1978).

Don M. Frick, *Greenleaf and Servant-Leader Listening* (Westfield, Indiana: The Greenleaf Center for Servant Leadership, 2011).

Viktor E. Frankl, *Man's Search for Meaning: An Introduction to Logotherapy* (New York: Pocket Books, 1963).

Daniel Goleman, Richard Boyatzis, and Annie McKee, *Primal Leadership: Learning to Lead with Emotional Intelligence* (Boston, Massachusetts: Harvard Business School Press, 2002).

Jill W. Graham, "Servant Leadership in Organizations: Inspirational and Moral," *Leadership Quarterly*, 2 (2), 105-119 (1991).

Robert Greene, *The 48 Laws of Power* (New York: Penguin Putnam Inc., 1998).

Robert K. Greenleaf, *Servant Leadership: A Journey into the Nature of Legitimate Power and Greatness* (New York: Paulist Press, 1977).

Robert K. Greenleaf, *The Institution as Servant* (Westfield, Indiana: The Greenleaf Center for Servant Leadership, 1972/2009).

Robert K. Greenleaf, *"The Leadership Crisis,"* in Larry Spears, ed., *The Power of Servant Leadership* (San Francisco: Berrett-Koehler Publishers, Inc., 1998).

Robert K. Greenleaf, *The Servant as Leader* (Westfield, Indiana: The Greenleaf Center for Servant Leadership, 1970/2008).

Robert K. Greenleaf, *Trustees as Servants* (Westfield, Indiana: The Greenleaf Center for Servant Leadership, 1974/2009).

John Hagell III, John Seely Brown, and Lang Davison, *The Power of Pull: How Small Moves, Smartly Made, Can Set Big Things in Motion* (New York: Basic Books, 2010).

David A. Heenan and Warren Bennis, *Co-Leaders: The Power of Great Partnerships* (New York: John Wiley & Sons, Inc., 1999).

John Heider, *The Tao of Leadership: Lao Tzu's Tao Te Ching Adapted for a New Age* (New York: Bantam Books, 1986).

Joseph Jaworski, *Synchronicity: The Inner Path of Leadership* (San Francisco: Berrett-Koehler Publishers, 1996).

Gospel of John (13:12-15), in *The Holy Bible, New International Version*, 1431-1432.

Kent M. Keith, *Do It Anyway: The Handbook for Finding Personal Meaning and Deep Happiness in a Crazy World* (Makawao, Maui, Hawaii: Inner Ocean Publishing, Inc., 2003).

Kent M. Keith, *Morality and Morale: A Business Tale* (Honolulu: Terrace Press, 2012).

Kent M. Keith, *The Silent Revolution: Dynamic Leadership in the Student Council* (Cambridge, Massachusetts: Harvard Student Agencies, Inc., 1968).

Daniel Kim, *Foresight as the Central Ethic of Leadership* (Westfield, Indiana: The Greenleaf Center for Servant Leadership, 2002).

James M. Kouzes and Barry Z. Posner, *A Leader's Legacy* (San Francisco: Jossey-Bass, 2006).

James M. Kouzes and Barry Z. Posner, *The Leadership Challenge* (Fourth Edition) (San Francisco: Jossey-Bass, 2007).

Richard Layard, *Happiness: Lessons from a New Science* (New York: The Penguin Press, 2005).

C. S. Lewis, *The Abolition of Man* (New York: The Macmillan Company, 1947).

Lao Tzu, *Tao Teh Ching*, trans. John C. H. Wu (Boston, Massachusetts: Shambhala, 2006).

Max Lerner, Introduction, *The Prince and The Discourses by Niccolo Machiavelli* (New York: The Modern Library, 1950).

Robert C. Liden, Sandy J. Wayne, Hao Zhao and David Henderson, "Servant Leadership: Development of a Multidimensional Measure and Multi-level Assessment," *The Leadership Quarterly*, 19, 161-177 (2008).

Isabel Lopez, "Finding Wisdom and Purpose in Chaotic Times," in Robert Banks and Kimberly Powell, eds., *Faith in Leadership* (San Francisco: Jossey-Bass, 2000).

Niccolo Machiavelli, *The Prince and the Discourses* (New York: The Modern Library, 1950).

Gospel of Matthew (20:25-28), in *The Holy Bible, New International Version* (Grand Rapids, Michigan: Zondervan Bible Publishers, 1978).

Ann McGee-Cooper and Gary Looper, *The Essentials of Servant Leadership: Principles in Practice* (Waltham, Massachusetts: Pegasus Communications, Inc., 2001).

Ann McGee-Cooper, Gary Looper, and Duane Trammell, *Being the Change: Profiles from Our Servant Leadership Learning Community* (Dallas, Texas: Ann McGee-Cooper and Associates, 2007).

Douglas McGregor, *The Human Side of Enterprise* (New York: McGraw-Hill, 1960/2006).

Ken Melrose, *Making the Grass Greener on Your Side: A CEO's Journey to Leading by Serving* (San Francisco: Berrett-Koehler Publishers, 1995).

Pastoral Institute, Columbus, Georgia, website: www.pilink.org

Dennis Prager, *Happiness Is a Serious Problem: A Human Nature Repair Manual* (New York: Regan Books, 1998).

Stephen Prosser, *Servant Leadership: More Philosophy, Less Theory* (Westfield, Indiana: The Greenleaf Center for Servant Leadership, 2010).

Steven B. Sample, *The Contrarian's Guide to Leadership* (San Francisco: Jossey-Bass, 2002).

Yasin Khalaf Sarayrah, "Servant leadership in the Bedouin-Arab culture," *Global Virtue Ethics Review*, Volume Five, Number 3, 58-79 (2004).

Peter M. Senge, "Robert Greenleaf's Legacy: A New Foundation for Twenty-First Century Institutions," in Larry C. Spears, ed., *Reflections on Leadership: How Robert K. Greenleaf's Theory of Servant Leadership Influenced Today's Top Management Thinkers* (New York: John Wiley & Sons, Inc. 1995).

James D. Showkeir, "The Business Case for Servant Leadership," in Larry C. Spears and Michele Lawrence, eds., *Focus on Leadership: Servant Leadership for the Twenty-First Century* (New York: John Wiley & Sons, Inc., 2002).

Larry C. Spears and Michele Lawrence, eds., *Focus on Leadership: Servant Leadership for the Twenty-First Century* (New York: John Wiley & Sons, Inc., 2002).

Larry Spears, ed., *Reflections on Leadership: How Robert K. Greenleaf's Theory of Servant Leadership Influenced Today's Top Management Thinkers* (New York: John Wiley & Sons, Inc. 1995).

Kenneth W. Thomas, *Intrinsic Motivation at Work: Building Energy and Commitment* (San Francisco: Berrett-Koehler Publishers, Inc., 2002).

Noel M. Tichy and Warren G. Bennis, *Judgment: How Winning Leaders Make Great Calls* (New York: The Penguin Group, 2007).

William B. Turner, *The Learning of Love: A Journey Toward Servant Leadership* (Macon, Georgia: Smyth & Helwys, 2000).

Dirk van Dierendonck, "Servant Leadership: A Review and Synthesis," *Journal of Management*, published online by Sage, 2 September 2010, at http://jom.sagepub.com/content/early/2010/09/01/0149206310380462.

Fred O. Walumbwa, Chad A. Hartnell and Adegoke Oke, "Servant Leadership, Procedural Justice Climate, Service Climate, Employee Attitudes, and Organizational Citizenship Behavior: A Cross-Level Investigation," *Journal of Applied Psychology*, Vol. 95, No. 3, 517-529 (2010).

Margaret J. Wheatley, *Leadership and the New Science* (San Francisco: Berrett-Koehler Publishers, Inc., 1994).

Margaret Wheatley, "The Work of the Servant-Leader," in Larry C. Spears and Michele Lawrence, eds., *Focus on Leadership: Servant Leadership for the Twenty-First Century* (New York: John Wiley & Sons, Inc., 2002).

David Whyte, *The Heart Aroused: Poetry and the Preservation of the Soul in Corporate America* (New York: Doubleday, 1994).

Andrew Wilson, ed., *World Scripture: A Comparative Anthology of Sacred Texts* (St. Paul, Minnesota: Paragon House, 1995).

Muhammad Yunus, *Creating a World Without Poverty* (New York: Public Affairs, 2007).

Notes

[1] Greenleaf, *Servant Leadership*, 13.

[2] Coles, *The Call of Service*, 69-70.

[3] Easwaran, *The Bhagavad Gita*, 76.

[4] Many of the quotations in this section are from Chapter 19, "Live for Others," in Wilson, *World Scripture*, 683-690.

[5] Lewis, *The Abolition of Man*, 115-116.

[6] Coles, *The Call of Service*, 75.

[7] Lao Tzu, *Tao Teh Ching*, 35.

[8] Heider, *The Tao of Leadership*, 33.

[9] Ezekiel (34: 2-10), in *The Holy Bible, New International Version*, 1153. The hadith of the Prophet Muhammed is quoted by Yasin Khalaf Sarayrah, in "Servant leadership in the Bedouin-Arab culture," *Global Virtue Ethics Review*, 75.

[10] Gospel of Matthew (20:25-28), in *The Holy Bible, New International Version*, 1318. See also Mark 10:42-45, page 1350.

[11] Gospel of John (13:12-15), in *The Holy Bible, New International Version*, 1431-1432.

[12] Greenleaf, *The Servant as Leader*, 15.

[13] Greenleaf, *The Institution as Servant*, 9.

[14] Spears, *Reflections on Leadership*, 4-7.

[15] Website of the Pastoral Institute, Columbus, Georgia: www.pilink.org.

[16] Liden, Wayne, Zhao, and Henderson, "Servant leadership: Development of a multidimensional measure and multi-level assessment," *The Leadership Quarterly*.

[17] Dirk van Dierendonck, "Servant Leadership: A Review and Synthesis," *Journal of Management*.

[18] Keith, *Do It Anyway*, 89.

[19] Tichy and Bennis, *Judgment*, 67-69.

[20] Greenleaf, *The Servant as Leader*, 9.

[21] The phrases "power model of leadership" and "service model of leadership" are mine, not Greenleaf's. They do not refer to theoretical models, but to a set of ideas or as-

sumptions that focus on leadership as an expression of personal power, on the one hand, and leadership as an opportunity for service, on the other hand. For example, Theory X would fit under the power model, while Theory Y and servant leadership would fit under the service model; "push" would fit under the power model, while "pull" would fit under the service model. See Douglas McGregor, *The Human Side of Enterprise*, and John Hagel III, John Seely Brown, and Lang Davison, *The Power of Pull*.

[22] Greenleaf, *The Servant as Leader*, 44.

[23] Lerner, Introduction, *The Prince* , xxx.

[24] Machiavelli, *The Prince*, 35.

[25] Id., 56.

[26] Id., 64.

[27] Id., 79.

[28] Greene, *The 48 Laws of Power*, xvii.

[29] Greenleaf, *The Institution as Servant*, 9.

[30] Ellis, *Founding Brothers*, 130.

[31] Autry, *The Servant Leader*, 21.

[32] Greenleaf, *The Servant as Leader*, 11-12.

[33] Greenleaf, "The Leadership Crisis," 87–88.

[34] Greenleaf, *The Servant as Leader*, 39.

[35] Id., 39-40.

[36] Turner, *The Learning of Love*, 158.

[37] Bordas, *Salsa, Soul, and Spirit*, 119.

[38] Id., 120.

[39] Id., 121.

[40] Wheatley, *The Work of the Servant-Leader*, 360-361.

[41] Blanchard, "Foreword: The Heart of Servant Leadership," xi.

[42] Blanchard, *Leading at a Higher Level*, 269.

[43] See Chapter 12, "Servant Leadership," by Ken Blanchard, Scott Blanchard, and Drea Zigarmi, in *Leading at a Higher Level*, 249-276.

44 Covey, "Foreword: Servant Leadership from the Inside Out," xi-xii.

45 Drucker, *The Effective Executive*, 52-53.

46 Senge, "Robert Greenleaf's Legacy: A New Foundation for Twenty-First Century Institutions," 217-218.

47 For the impacts of servant leadership in the workplace, the following articles are available: Mark G. Ehrhart, "Leadership and procedural justice climate as antecedents of unit-level organizational citizenship behavior, *Personnel Psychology*, 57, 61-94 (2004); Robert C. Liden, Sandy J. Wayne, Hao Zhao, and David Henderson, "Servant leadership: Development of a multidimensional measure and multilevel assessment," *Leadership Quarterly*, 19, 161-177 (2008); D. M. Mayer, M. Bardes, and R. F. Piccolo, " Do servant-leaders help satisfy follower needs? An organizational justice perspective," *European Journal of Work and Organizational Psychology*, 17, 180-197 (2008); M. J. Neubert, K.M. Kacmar, D. S. Carlson, L. B. Chonko, & J.A. Roberts, "Regulatory focus as a mediator of the influence of initiating structure and servant leadership on employee behavior, *Journal of Applied Psychology*, 93(6), 1220-1233 (2008); R. F. Piccolo and J. A. Colquitt, "Transformational leadership and job behaviors: The mediating role of core job characteristics," *Academy of Management Journal*, 49, 327-340 (2006); and Fred O. Walumbwa, Chad A. Hartnell, & Adegoke Oke, "Servant leadership, procedural justice climate, service climate, employee attitudes, and organizational citizenship behavior: A cross-level investigation, *Journal of Applied Psychology*, 95, 517-529 (2010).

48 Personal communication with Jack Lowe, Jr., August 20, 2007. The quote is a variation of a quote found in Ann McGee-Cooper and Gary Looper, *The Essentials of Servant Leadership: Principles in Practice*, 9.

49 Kouzes and Posner, *A Leader's Legacy*, 64.

50 Goleman, Boyatzis, and McKee, *Primal Leadership*, 8-9.

51 Lopez, "Finding Wisdom and Purpose in Chaotic Times," 85-86.

52 Greenleaf, *The Servant as Leader*, 18. See also Don M. Frick, *Greenleaf and Servant-Leader Listening.*

53 Id., 16.

54 Yunus, *Creating a World Without Poverty*, 45–47.

55 Greenleaf, *The Institution as Servant*, 23-24.

56 Turner, *The Learning of Love*,151.

57 Blanchard, *Leading at a Higher Level*, 250.

58 Sample, *The Contrarian's Guide to Leadership*, 121.

59 Id., 121-122.

[60] Autry, *The Servant Leader,* 20.

[61] Greenleaf, *The Servant as Leader,* 15.

[62] Greenleaf, *Servant Leadership,* 154–159.

[63] Drucker, *The Effective Executive,* 59.

[64] Id., 60.

[65] Showkeir, "The Business Case for Servant Leadership," 158.

[66] Id.

[67] Kouzes and Posner, *A Leader's Legacy,* 79.

[68] Autry, *The Servant Leader,* 20-21.

[69] Quoted in Ann McGee-Cooper and Gary Looper, *The Essentials of Servant Leadership: Principles in Practice,* 11.

[70] Barnard, *The Functions of the Executive,* 165.

[71] Personal communication with Jack Lowe, Jr., August 20, 2007.

[72] Wheatley, *Leadership and the New Science,* 38-39.

[73] Covey, "Foreword: Servant Leadership from the Inside Out," xi-xii.

[74] Ebener, *The Servant Parish.*

[75] Quoted in a TDIndustries brochure. Found also in McGee-Cooper, Looper, and Trammell, *Being the Change,* 14-15.

[76] Showkeir, "The Business Case for Servant Leadership," 160-161.

[77] Behar, *It's Not About the Coffee,* 55.

[78] Thomas, *Intrinsic Motivation at Work,* 44.

[79] Kouzes and Posner, *The Leadership Challenge,* 115.

[80] Melrose, *Making The Grass Greener On Your Side,* 6.

[81] Greenleaf, *The Servant as Leader,* 25.

[82] Id., 26.

[83] Id., 27.

[84] Kim, *Foresight as the Central Ethic of Leadership,* 3.

85 Id.

86 Collins, *Good to Great*, 65-69.

87 Tichy and Bennis, *Judgment*, 157-159.

88 Jaworski, *Synchronicity*, 182.

89 De Pree, *Leadership Is an Art*, 14-15.

90 Keith, *The Silent Revolution*, 11.

91 Thomas, *Intrinsic Motivation at Work*, 46.

92 Id., 22.

93 Frankl, *Man's Search for Meaning*, 154.

94 Deci, *Why We Do What We Do*, 128.

95 Layard, *Happiness: Lessons from a New Science*, 22.

96 Prager, *Happiness Is a Serious Problem*, 101.

97 Baker and Stauth, *What Happy People Know*, 21.

98 Ben-Shahar, *Happier: Learn the Secrets to Daily Joy and Lasting Fulfillment*, 33.

99 Id., 33-39.

100 Greenleaf, *Servant Leadership*, 329-330.

101 Whyte, *The Heart Aroused*, 117-118.

102 Greenleaf, *Servant Leadership*, 329.

103 Id., 88.

104 See, for example, Jill W. Graham, "Servant leadership in organizations: Inspirational and moral," *Leadership Quarterly*; Mark G. Ehrhart, "Leadership and procedural justice climate as antecedents of unit-level organizational citizenship behavior, *Personnel Psychology*; Robert C. Liden, Sandy J. Wayne, Hao Zhao, and David Henderson, "Servant leadership: Development of a multidimensional measure and multilevel assessment," *Leadership Quarterly*; Fred O. Walumbwa, Chad A. Hartnell, and Adegoke Oke, "Servant leadership, procedural justice climate, service climate, employee attitudes, and organizational citizenship behavior: A cross-level investigation, *Journal of Applied Psychology*.

105 Burns, *Leadership*, 4.

106 Id., 20.

[107] Collins, *Good to Great*, 21.

[108] Id., 28.

[109] Id., 30.

[110] Block, *Stewardship: Choosing Service Over Self-Interest*, xx.

[111] Id., 10.

[112] Heenan and Bennis, *Co-Leaders*, 3.

[113] Id., 5–12.

Acknowledgments

I would like to thank those who commented on the first edition of the book while it was being written: Dr. Carolyn Crippen, Charley Bellinger, Jerry Glashagel, Dr. Dan Ebener, Dr. Stuart Gothold, Rev. Dan Hatch, Dr. John Horsman, Gary Kent, Isabel Lopez, Geneva Loudd, Jack Lowe, Jr., Dr. Ann McGee-Cooper, Dr. Fran Newman, Richard Pieper, Kay Stone, Christine Van Meter, Ed Voerman, Dr. Margit Watts, and my wife, Dr. Elizabeth Keith. My thanks to those who reviewed and commented on the second edition: Phil Anderson, Dolores Jones, Courtney Knies, Isabel Lopez, and Dr. Ann McGee-Cooper. I am grateful to them all for the gift of their time and insight.

About the Author

Dr. Kent M. Keith has been an attorney, state government official, high tech park developer, university president, YMCA executive, and full-time speaker and author. From 2007 to 2012 he served as the Chief Executive Officer of the Greenleaf Center for Servant Leadership in Indiana.

Dr. Keith earned a B.A. in Government from Harvard University, an M.A. in Philosophy and Politics from Oxford University in England, a Certificate in Japanese from Waseda University in Tokyo, a J.D. from the University of Hawaii, and an Ed. D. from the University of Southern California. He is a Rhodes Scholar.

Dr. Keith is known throughout the world as the author of the Paradoxical Commandments, which he first published in 1968 in a booklet for student leaders. During the past ten years he has published four books about the commandments, including *Anyway: The Paradoxical Commandments*, which became a national bestseller and was translated into 17 languages. He is also the author of three books on servant leadership: *The Case for Servant Leadership; Servant Leadership in the Boardroom: Fulfilling the Public Trust;* and *Questions and Answers about Servant Leadership.*

Over the years, Dr. Keith has given more than 1,000 presentations, conference papers, and seminars on a wide variety of topics in the United States and eight countries in Europe and Asia. His current presentations and seminars are focused on servant leadership, the Paradoxical Commandments, finding personal meaning at home and at work, and the positive impact of morality in the workplace. He has been featured on the front page of *The New York Times* and in *People* magazine, *The Washington Post*, *The San Francisco Chronicle*, and *Family Circle*. He was interviewed by Katie Couric on NBC's *Today Show* and by Dr. Robert H. Schuller on *The Hour of Power*. He has been quoted in *The Wall Street Journal* and *Inc.com*. He has appeared on dozens of TV shows and more than 100 radio programs in the United States, the United Kingdom, Japan, Korea, and Australia.

More information about Dr. Keith and his work is available at www.kentmkeith.com. He may be contacted at: drkentkeith@hotmail.com.

Other books by Dr. Kent M. Keith

Servant Leadership:

Questions and Answers about Servant Leadership
by Kent M. Keith
(Greenleaf Center for Servant Leadership, 2012)

During the past two decades, Dr. Keith has given hundreds of speeches and workshops on servant leadership. This book shares the questions that he is often asked and the answers that he gives when he is making presentations. In some cases, the answers have been expanded for this publication. This book will be especially useful to those who naturally begin with questions, whether they are new to servant leadership or have been on the journey for many years. The book provides the reader with starting points for further study, reflection, and implementation. Where applicable, answers conclude with recommendations for additional reading. A list of all the recommended readings can be found at the end of the text.
Available from www.toservefirst.com

Servant Leadership in the Boardroom: Fulfilling the Public Trust
by Kent M. Keith
(Greenleaf Center for Servant Leadership, 2011)

This book presents and augments the views of Robert Greenleaf on the opportunity of board members of all types of corporations—for-profit and non-profit—to truly lead and make a difference for their organizations and those their organizations serve. The book provides historical background on the public purpose of all corporations, the responsibilities of board members as trustees for the public good, the unique value of board judgments, the relationship between the board and administration, and keys to board effectiveness, including the board as a "council of equals" that focuses on what matters most, asking fundamental questions and seeking information about how well the organization is serving its employees and society at large.
Available from www.toservefirst.com

Morality and Morale: A Business Tale
by Kent M. Keith
(Terrace Press, 2012)

Morality and Morale: A Business Tale is a story about a young business manager faced with a moral dilemma at work. As he calls on others for advice, he learns that business is a way to serve others; that there is a universal moral code that each of us can follow in our businesses and our private lives; that morality and morale are related, so that when morality goes up, so does morale; that treating others right can be a source of personal energy and can result in business success; and that living morally makes life more meaningful. The book includes Notes for the Reader with background on the ideas introduced in the story. **Available from www.moralityandmorale.com**

Paradoxical Commandments:

Anyway: The Paradoxical Commandments
by Kent M. Keith
(G. P. Putnam's Sons, 2002).

The Paradoxical Commandments were first written by Kent Keith in 1968, when he was 19, as part of a booklet for student leaders. The commandments subsequently spread around the world, and have been used by millions of people. This book is an introduction to the Paradoxical Commandments and what they mean. It was a national bestseller in the United States, and has been translated into 17 languages.
Available from www.paradoxicalcommandments.com

Do It Anyway: Finding Personal Meaning and Deep Happiness by Living the Paradoxical Commandments
by Kent M. Keith
(Inner Ocean Publishing, 2003; New World Library, 2008).

This book is a companion to *Anyway: The Paradoxical Commandments*. It describes how people have used the Paradoxical Commandments to break away from their daily excuses, or a painful past, or a complicated present, to find meaning anyway. This is a practical "how to" book for those who want to put the Paradoxical Commandments into practice in their own lives. The book includes forty stories about people who are living the commandments; questions for personal reflection and group discussion; and an interview with the author in which he answers the questions he is asked most often about the commandments.
Available from www.paradoxicalcommandments.com

Jesus Did It Anyway: The Paradoxical Commandments for Christians
by Kent M. Keith
(G. P. Putnam's Sons, 2005).

For more than forty years, the Paradoxical Commandments have been used by Christians all over the globe. Mother Teresa thought they were important enough to put on the wall of her children's home in Calcutta. *Jesus Did It Anyway* illustrates the Paradoxical Commandments through stories and verses from both the Old Testament and the New Testament, the teachings of Jesus and the apostles, and personal anecdotes. The 14-chapter book includes a study guide with questions for each chapter.
Available from www.paradoxicalchristians.com

Have Faith Anyway: The Vision of Habakkuk for Our Times
by Kent M. Keith
(Jossey-Bass, 2008).

Have Faith Anyway explores the author's new eleventh Paradoxical Commandment: *The world is full of violence, injustice, starvation, disease, and environmental destruction. Have faith anyway.* To help the reader better understand what it is like to have faith in the face of seemingly insurmountable problems, the author tells the story of the Old Testament prophet Habakkuk, whose vision of a conversation with God led him to an inspiring affirmation of faith even in the face of devastation and death. The book concludes with the author's own vision of a conversation between a Christian and God today. The book includes a Readers Guide for Reflection and Study.
Available from www.paradoxicalchristians.com

High School Student Council Leadership:

The Silent Revolution: Dynamic Leadership in the Student Council
by Kent M. Keith
(Harvard Student Agencies, 1968; Terrace Press, 2003)

This is the book for which Dr. Keith wrote the Paradoxical Commandments, 149 words that have spread all over the world and have been used by millions of people of all ages and backgrounds. The book was first published in 1968, when Dr. Keith was 19, a sophomore in college. In the book, Keith encourages student leaders to work together, through the system, to achieve positive, lasting change. He believes that students councils can, and should, make a difference. He explains the need to love people, and do what is meaningful and satisfying, whether you get credit or not. He uses hypothetical stories to describe practical leadership skills and dilemmas, argues that the "good guys" can win, and urges students to take action now. "Don't vegetate," he says. "Initiate."
Available from www.paradoxicalcommandments.com

The Silent Majority: The Problem of Apathy and the Student Council
by Kent M. Keith
(National Association of Secondary School Principals, 1971; Terrace Press, 2004)

Dr. Keith was 20, a junior in college, when he wrote this book as a companion to his first book, *The Silent Revolution: Dynamic Leadership in the Student Council*. Keith says: *"The Silent Majority* is written from high school student council leaders who want to give the student council its noblest meaning and purpose: people helping people." Keith argues that no one is completely apathetic—everyone is interested in *something*. It's up to student leaders to find out what their fellow students are interested in, and then link up with those interests. In the process, student leaders will learn more about themselves, and discover the richness of life that is available to those who become "people people."
Available from www.paradoxicalcommandments.com

Made in the USA
Lexington, KY
16 September 2017